TO: Rici

MAY GOD BLESS YOU

AND YOUR FAMILY

Henry L Walker

Nov - 2019

BROTHER TO BROTHER

KEVAN L. WAITERS

BROTHER TO BROTHER
THE MIRACLE OF FAMILY

TATE PUBLISHING & Enterprises

Published by Tate Publishing & Enterprises, LLC
127 E. Trade Center Terrace | Mustang, Oklahoma 73064 USA
1.888.361.9473 | www.tatepublishing.com

Tate Publishing is committed to excellence in the publishing industry. The company reflects the philosophy established by the founders, based on Psalm 68:11,
"The Lord gave the word and great was the company of those who published it."

Book design copyright © 2010 by Tate Publishing, LLC. All rights reserved.
Cover design by Chris Webb
Interior design by Jeff Fisher

Published in the United States of America
ISBN: 978-1-61663-344-8
1. Biography & Autobiography, Personal Memoirs
2. Religion, Christian Life, Family
10.05.10

Dedication

From Kevan Waiters

If there is one man in this world I would pattern my life after, do whatever he told me and listen to every word he said, that man would be my father, Harry Lee Waiters. Standing right beside him would be my mother, Carrie Lee Moses-Waiters. Every child born into this world needs the guidance, love, and disciplining hand of a strong father figure in his life.

My dad was my mentor.

My dad was my best friend.

My dad was indeed a counselor to many.

My dad was a man after the things of God.

My dad was a man of godly wisdom.

He showed me by example, and for that I will always love and appreciate him.

He always told me, "Son, vengeance belongs to the Lord. There is no need to fight; the battle is the Lord's."

One of my dad's favorite sayings was this: "Don't confuse me with the facts, because my mind is already made up."

To my mom: You have been a warrior for all of us. In the midst of adversity, you were the glue that held us together. You proved your love to us by getting in the trenches with us. You are a faithful mom, a mom full of faith. You're our beacon in the night and visionary for the family at all times.

Mother, I extend with all gratitude from the bottom of my heart, a sincere thank you.

I want to personally give a special thank-you to Veronica Mayfield, who tirelessly contributed to this project in a major way.

DEDICATION FROM D. FRANK WAITERS

In my early days, while I was living in Washington, DC, Reverend Colon Johnson, a former pastor, came to my aid and assisted me by giving me his 1977 Plymouth. I was able to get around and make some money for myself. It might not seem like much to many, but I was able to continue the taxicab business he started. I was able to go to church, follow my pastor, and hear the Word. Because of his help in the beginning, I have been in the ministry now for twenty years.

To the nurses, doctors, and staff at the NIH, VA, and Washington Hospitals.

To the transplant team, I really thank you.

To the dialysis center I used for my treatment, I know I was a handful, but I thank you.

To another pastor friend of mine, Pastor John Griffin, who witnessed some of my dark hours and stayed right there by my side. I came home from one of my hospital visits to an empty house. No furniture, even—we had to sleep on the floor. He stayed by my side and helped me until times got better. I just want to say thank you.

To my sister, Denise, you were so sweet to offer me your kidney. I know how much you love your brother. Thank you.

To all of my brothers: Joe, Larry, Ernest, and Kevan—you guys are the greatest brothers anyone can ask for.

To all of my sisters I haven't mentioned yet: Carolyn, Janice, Irene, and that baby girl, Ginger, you all have been a delight to me, and I just want to say thank you.

To my children and my beautiful wife, Nita, if you only knew just how much you mean to me. You have been a source of strength, and I thank you.

However, no one takes the place of Momma. Thank you, Momma, for everything you've done for me.

I don't want to leave out Mickey. He was given to me when I was a month old, and he lived to be 14 years old.

Let me leave these words with you. God has given us a renewed hope. What He's done for me, He will do for you. I hope you find inspiration in what God did for my brother, our family, and me. Thank you for allowing us to come into your automobiles, your homes, and your offices—wherever you might be reading this. There is hope.

FOREWORD

Every child who comes into the world is a gift from God. The gender and ethnicity of that child is determined by the creative and ingenious mind of our Creator. He fills each one with capabilities, talents, and special gifts designed to enhance this universe. Each is unique in his or her special way. Having been blessed with eleven gifts from God, I adopt this sentiment as my own. The development of this book will reveal some highs and lows of parenting, some good times and some stressful times as families find themselves in different situations. But the greatest thing revealed in the pages of this book is a never doubting, always believing in the glorious power of God.

I, Carrie Lee Moses-Waiters, am the mother of the two sons you will read about in this book. The strings of my heart have never been stretched so far as they were during this time in our lives, and right now, all I can say is, "God, you've been good to me."

I was reared in an era when the bonds of family were as strong as a three-fold cord, not quickly broken. A mother cared for the family from sun up to sun down without complaining and was more protective of her family than a mother hen was over hers. Much time was spent in prayer. Whenever trouble was about, you got down on your knees, and you had a little talk with Jesus. He would let you know everything will be all right. He did it then, and He's still doing it today.

He is the same God, yesterday, today and forever.

May God bless you continually!

Acknowledgments

It is difficult, at best, to remember every little detail or input given that made this undertaking a success. First and foremost, I thank God. Without Him, none of this would be possible. Even the reason we are able to write this book is due to the undeniable, creative power of God.

I thank Him for the very experience that led to this opportunity.

My brother Donald Frank is at the top of the list of people that I take my hat off to. He allowed me to be a benefactor of life for him. Because of him, I've seen more of what God will do if you just believe. I thank my mother, who at first was reluctant to allow my brother and me to go through this medical procedure, but just like I knew she would, she gave it to God in prayer and gave us her blessing. You always want your mom on your side.

Melvette, Brandon, and Keri—thank you. To my sisters: Irene, Janice, Carolyn, Denise, and Ginger—I know you love me. My brothers who I haven't mentioned, Ernest, Joe Ray, Larry, Jim, and Ollie—I thank all of you guys for your love and support. To my brother, Harry, who is at home with the Lord, I was able to relive some memories of you while doing this project; you could always make us laugh.

Ken Bell, thanks for your help in getting this project started.

TABLE OF CONTENTS

INTRODUCTION

I come to you at a place and time in my life when things have finally begun to settle down. I have returned to my home in South Carolina from my stint in the military, but I am still on active reserve status. I am blessed to have seen some places perhaps some will never see. I have traveled to some of the world's most remote places—so remote that I was told, "The further you go in any particular direction, and you will see human beings that we know as head hunters and cannibals." Suffice it to say, I didn't go any further.

The military afforded me opportunities that I may not have gotten otherwise, but I have always been a hard worker, so maybe I would have. From my youth, our father instilled values and morals in each of his children, and with his instruction, we had the tools to head out in the right direction.

I was back in Lancaster, South Carolina, to be near my mother. She is getting on in age, and I wanted to be close by, so whatever she needs, I will make sure, if it were at all possible, she would have it. I was doing pretty well, no complaints. I was back home near mother, working as a detective at the Lancaster County sheriff's office and going back and forth to Greenville, S.C. doing my reserve work. Life was good.

Then, I got this phone call—"Brother, will you give me ...?"— and another chapter of my life began. Knowing the love my mother has for all her children, the fact that she had already lost one son, my mother's humble beginning, and what she and her family endured to protect the children and the livelihood of us all, it wasn't even an issue. I didn't even have to think about it: The answer was, "Yes."

I take you now to the beginning, so you will further understand how I made the decision without regard to my own welfare. And you know what? Life is better now than I would have ever imagined.

THE SIGNIFICANCE
OF THREE

I'm not into numerology or anything like that, but it is amazing how events of my life and my family members' lives happened in threes, or had the number three involved somehow. Of course, I recognize the greatest three of them all: the Father, the Son, and the Holy Ghost, to whom we give the credit for our very existence.

The number three is the basic foundation for this book. From early on in life up to the present, the number three has been very significant. Some of the events are more significant than others, but they all center on the number three.

The first greatest as I stated before, is God: the Father, the Son, and the Holy Ghost. Nothing compares to those three. I simply have to say it—God is awesome. For Him to do what He did in my body is nothing short of a miracle. We are all familiar with the story of Eve, how she came into existence. God caused Adam to fall into a deep sleep while He performed a little surgery on him, and when he awakened, he was one rib short. The rest, as they say, is history. I don't know when God did what He did inside me. All I know is when I was x-rayed prior to my surgery, I only had two kidneys, but the day of my surgery, they took one last X-ray, and there were three kidneys.

God has a way of showing up when you least expect it. Remember Shadrach, Meshach, and Abednego? The soldier said, "Did not we throw three men in the furnace? But I see four and He looks like the Son of God."

I am glad God showed up and did a little rearranging in me. I can't tell you *when* He did it. I can't tell you *how* He did it. All I can tell you is *that* He did it. I have to tell you like the young man in the Bible who was blind from birth told everybody when they kept asking him how he received his sight.

The story goes something like this: Jesus and His disciples were walking along, and they saw a man blind from birth. The disciples asked, "Master, who did sin that this man is born blind, him or his parents?"

Jesus responded, "Neither he nor his parents, but that the power of God could be demonstrated."

It will blow you away to see what Jesus did next. He spit on the ground and made a little mud from the spittle and smoothed the mud over the blind man's eyes. Then, He told him to go and wash in the Pool of Siloam. The man went where he was sent and did what he was told. He walked away blind and came back with sight.

As the story goes on, the Pharisees were trying to find fault in Jesus because He said, "He was the Son of God," and they didn't believe. When they saw the man, who they all knew as the blind beggar, was no longer blind, they asked him, "What happened to you, who did this to you?"

He told them, "A man called Jesus."

The Pharisees said, "This man called Jesus is evil."

A few more words were exchanged between them.

The man said, "Whether He is good or whether He is evil, I don't know, but I do know this: Whereas I once was blind, but now I see."

All this man knew was that God showed up, and all I know is this: I went to bed with two kidneys, and I woke up with three.

God showed up.

A Mother's Love: The Beginning

Carrie Lee Moses-Waiters

"Harry, we're pregnant again."

Family means the world to me, and I wanted to be surrounded by as much family as I could. Bringing life into the world is as much a miracle as God Himself stepping out into nothing and saying, "Let there be light." Every child I birthed into this world is a miracle to me, and each one is unique in their own way.

As for me, I was born March 23, 1922, so I had a real appreciation for family. My mother and father had eleven children, of which I am the sixth. There were eight girls and three boys, so as you might imagine, things were a little tight sometimes. Life got pretty special sometimes.

We owned a wagon buggy; back then it was our means of transportation. In 1925, I saw my first automobile, and I was about thirteen years old before we had a car to ride in. We called them automobiles, not cars. It was a 1929 "A" model Ford. The cheapest I ever saw gas was seven cents a gallon. Then it came to twelve cents and then twenty-one cents; it was going on up.

Back then, we had cows, so we didn't have to buy milk. We had our own hogs, which we killed, so we had our own meat and lard and things like that. We raised wheat and made our own flour, so the only things we had to buy were things like sugar.

It sure was something to watch our daddy cut the wheat down, and he would carry it to a place in Monroe, North Carolina, where they made the flour. We had plain flour. You had to add soda and baking powder to it. Sometimes, we would swap some of our flour and get self-rising flour. Everybody did some bartering every now and then.

When I was picking cotton, you'd make fifty cents per hundred pounds. If you wanted to make a dollar, you had to pick 200 pounds.

We were a big family. Sometimes we'd have eight or ten bales of cotton. We made forty dollars for a bale of cotton. We'd pick all day. We'd go down in the field about six o'clock, or seven at the latest, so we could get a sack full of dew cotton. Some people would pick 150 pounds.

From when I was about fifteen years old up until the time I got married, I was picking about 200 pounds of cotton a day so I could make two dollars. Don't fret too much about the money exchange; the value of ten dollars then was like $500 now.

If I go to the store now to get a can of dressed salmon, I can get that for about $1.50 a can. Back in my childhood, I'd pay ten cents a can.

When I started school, we walked about six or eight miles one way; there wasn't a school bus. Our school had two rooms. I don't know if it was fifty students or less than fifty students, but we only had two teachers. Each one taught a group. One had the group from elementary to the third grade, while the other one taught third grade to the seventh grade.

It was the same way about church. We had to walk to church. Then, in late 1939 or early 1940, we got an automobile, and we could ride to church.

I met my husband, Harry Lee Waiters, at the church. We went to the same church, New Hope Baptist Church. It was founded in 1857. It was a little wooden church back then. Now, we've got a brick building.

I've been going to that church for 75 years.

Harry Lee and I got married September 6, 1941. We have eleven children.

Our first child was born June 7, 1942. In 1943, the second child was born. The third child was born in 1945, the fourth child in 1947, fifth in 1949, sixth in 1952, seventh in 1954, eighth in 1956, ninth in 1957, tenth in 1963, and the eleventh in 1964. I had seven children born at home and four born in the hospital.

I had a midwife for five—Ernest, Irene, Janice, D. Frank, and Joe. Ernest was seven pounds. Irene was nine pounds. Janice was ten pounds, D. Frank was thirteen and a half pounds, and Joe was eight pounds.

Dr. Clinton came to deliver Carolyn. She was nine pounds. My mother delivered Larry. He was seven pounds.

Dr. Horton delivered Denise, then Kevan, Ginger, and Harry, all at the hospital. I only wanted to have two children, a boy and a girl, and I wanted the boy to be the oldest. My husband wanted eight. We had his eight and my two, which were ten. Then the Lord gave us the last one, Harry, which made eleven.

In World War II, my husband was supposed to go to war, but he went to Columbia, South Carolina. They kept him down there a week. He could have gone on and served, but he came home.

It would have been hard on me with two children and my husband gone to war.

Schools were still segregated when the oldest ones started. Ernest, Irene, Janice, and D. Frank all walked to school about three miles from home. They went to Mount Carmel Elementary School. D. Frank went there for six weeks. Then, he went to Oak Ridge. Then, children started riding the bus.

The children from Joe to Harry never walked to school; they all rode the bus.

I was secretary of the PTA at their schools, Hillside Elementary and Hillside High School in Heath Springs. Six of my children graduated from Hillside: Ernest, Irene, Janice, D. Frank, Joe, and Carolyn.

I was involved in school the years those six children were there. Then, we had the district PTA with other counties. After they graduated, integration began. The PTA was cut out. Hillside didn't have it anymore. It wasn't functional.

I visited all of the schools where my children attended. Later, I worked in the school cafeteria.

As time progressed I didn't see any difference between blacks and whites in the schools. The teachers and principals would be different. It was more of a problem with them being integrated not the students. I worked for Mr. Kirkland at McDonald Green and Miss Nancy Crockett at Rice Elementary. Those were the only two white schools where I worked. I got along well with the principals and teachers.

I started working in the school system after I had five children. Then, I'd come home and farm.

Cotton was the main product. We also had corn; we made our own molasses, and raised our own hogs and cows. We used to milk the cows. All the children down to Kevan milked the cows in the morning before they went to school and again in the evening when they came home.

We used mules to plow until we got our first tractor about 1969.

D. Frank was a good student. He was the valedictorian of his class. He still didn't study like he needed to study. His teacher told him if he'd go to college, they'd pay him to go to school. He knew mathematics. He was smart in school, but he just played around.

I always wanted to go on and further my education. My children had a chance to go on further. They got to ride the bus. They didn't have to walk like I did. My husband and I decided if they wanted to go on to college, we'd make every effort to send them. Ernest and Irene went to college. We worked hard and borrowed money from the bank and sent them to college. Then, Janice went. In her second year of college, D. Frank started. That was four in college. Then come Joe—he was the fifth—and Carolyn, sixth. Every one of my children had an opportunity to go further than I did. Some of them finished and others didn't but they all had an opportunity to go. When Ginger and Harry were born, Ernest and Irene were in college.

The Lord just blessed me. I knew education was important. I would do anything we needed to do to try to make it possible for them to go; we'd try to make it happen. That meant working in the field and on the job. My husband worked in the field and on the job. It took dedication and commitment for us to do that, but we worked together on it. We were in agreement with raising our children.

Harry Lee got his first automobile—his own car—in 1947. It was a Chevrolet. I first got a television in 1954. I would always go to the theater on Saturday and see the Westerns. I was carrying Ernest, Irene, Janice, D. Frank, Joe, and Carolyn. My husband would take us to the show every Saturday at eleven o'clock. He'd help me upstairs with the children, and he'd come back later. He didn't go to the theater. Then when Larry came along, we had seven children. For the adults, it cost eleven cents to go to the theater, and for children, it was a nickel.

Larry was born on the thirteenth of December, and that Christmas, Harry Lee got me a television. It had a combination of television, radio, and record player. I haven't been back to the theater since then.

The first time I got a telephone was in the 1960s. We had what was known as a party line. There would be four or five parties on the line. If one family was using it, you just had to wait until the line was clear before you could use it.

I never tried to tie the line up, but some people would get on there and talk thirty minutes, knowing it was a party line. Sometimes you had to get on there and ask, "Would y'all please let me use the phone?" Sometimes they would be kind of rude, and sometimes they'd hang up, but that's the way it was. Frank complained there were too many people on the line, so we eventually got a private line.

My son Joe sent me the money and told me to pay down on a color television. I told him there was nothing wrong with the black and white one, but he said, "Momma, if you get this television, you'll like it. You won't want the black and white." Sure enough, I got that television. That was during the time of the Vietnam War—about 1967.

I had been married for forty-two years when Harry Lee passed away. When two people love each other, they communicate with each other and pray together. If you pray together, you can stay together. It's communication for the husband and the wife. Whatever was to be done, we discussed it. That really keeps a family together. You've got to be together on keeping the family together. You've got to understand one another.

People need more communication. Today, the wife has a job and the husband has a job. They each have their own bank account. They aren't communicating like they were when we were young. The lady has her own thing. Even if they are both working, she thinks it's his job to do everything. That's the way they do it now, a lot of them. She buys what she wants and does what she wants to do.

Twenty years later my son, Ernest, had to go to Vietnam, and then my son, D. Frank. When D. Frank was in college, he got a job with Eastern Airlines. He had been in college one year. I told him he better go back to college, because if they found him not in college, he'd have to go like his brother did.

He said, "No." Sure enough, he had to go into service.

D. Frank did his basic training in Fort Bragg, and they sent him to Columbia—Fort Jackson—and then to Vietnam. When I learned he was on his way to Vietnam, it was the worst thing I could have heard.

I had two sons, a son-in-law, and a nephew serving in Vietnam. I had four over there at the same time.

The only communication was from the letters they wrote. There was no big media coverage to tell us what was going on. Ernest Lee went to Vietnam on a ship, but D. Frank flew over there. I didn't know they were sending him like that because he had just come out of basic training.

My husband told me, "You have to stop worrying about that, because when they come out of basic training, they go right on in there."

I asked the Lord to let him come back home. He showed me Frank would come back home, and that's what happened.

Ernest, D. Frank and Joe were drafted, but Kevan decided to join the Marines in 1976. I didn't feel as badly as I did with Ernest, D. Frank, and Joe, because that was Kevan's choice to volunteer. I wasn't afraid like I was when Ernest and his brothers went in the service. Knowing the Lord and knowing He was on my side assured me everything was all right. When Kevan went in, I asked Him for the same thing. I asked Him to take care of Kevan wherever he went, wherever it was. I knew the Lord was with him, and he was going to come back home.

For us, things got better as the children grew older. I just had the two youngest still at home. I was getting older and didn't have to worry too much. Life seemed to be much better, but we were still farming.

When Harry graduated from high school, my husband was sick. Ginger was in her second year of college, so I continued to pay her way. It made a difference because all of the others were grown. The older ones all had families of their own. I didn't look to them for anything, but I haven't suffered since my husband died because my children are there for me.

My husband had insurance on all of us through the company he was working for, while he was working. When he died, they told me that I wouldn't have any more support from him. After then, the insurance went sky-high, and I didn't have the money to get it. Some of my medicine is $116 just for thirty little tablets and a hundred-something dollars just for the eye drops. When you don't have insurance, it's rough on you. I don't have anything but Medicare. You can outlive your insurance. When you are eighty or eighty-five, you don't have the money to buy insurance.

THE STRINGS OF A MOTHER'S HEART

It really bothered me when D. Frank had to go on dialysis. He was on that and using a home remedy. I really didn't know he was as sick as he was until he went to the hospital, and then I went to Washington to see him. He had deteriorated so much. He had lost so much weight. He could hardly walk. As heavy as he had been, he only weighed about 110 or 115 pounds, and that really hit my heartstrings.

He told me he was ready to go home to be with the Lord.

I told him, "No, God isn't ready for you yet. You've got more work to do."

I learned the dialysis wouldn't continue to prolong his life, and they began talk of him needing another procedure done, or he would die. It wasn't the first time the doctors had told him that. They kept it hush-hush because they thought I'd be worried about it. Then, out of emotion and love for her brother, one of my daughters, Denise, said, "You can have my kidney."

When it came down to it, all of my children were eager to give him a kidney. We later found out only one was a perfect match. My son, Joe, thought he was supposed to give him a kidney because he was next to him in age, but it didn't work like that. Kevan's kidney was a perfect match, even though D. Frank was ten years older than Kevan.

As a mother, you can't explain to people what it's like to go through something like that. It's hard, but then you've got to have God on your side. Things will come into your mind to try and shake your faith. The devil kept saying, "Well, you're going to have two sons on the operating table; both of them could die." That went through my mind. I asked the Lord to take care of that and He did.

I was even scared to ride the elevator in the hospital. That's the only elevator I ever got on. D. Frank was on the 11th floor in the hospital, and when it came time to take on that eleventh floor, I got in that elevator and I went on up there. That elevator would talk and say, "You're on the first floor. You're on the second floor." All the way, it talked to me, and I didn't get afraid. It was like I was in a cloud or something.

They were doing the blood work for the operation but had to stop because D. Frank had a sore on his leg. That doctor was a man of God, because he told me, "I'm not going to do an operation until D. Frank is strong enough to live through it, and we find out what's causing the sore on his leg."

During this ordeal, I learned more people than me were praying for my sons. One of the prayer partners revealed to Kevan that the Lord had shown her he would be pierced on his right side. Now I know the Lord had intervened; that's why he showed that vision. I felt good the Lord was openly revealing about this situation to the prayer partners. Miss Ross, who worked at the local telephone company, said her sister had a vision that Kevan would be pierced on his right side.

She also stated that God told her, "He could hardly bear it when they hung His Son on the cross, that they had pierced His Son on the right side, His Son had an open wound for mankind, and His Son would live and not die."

It was a relief to me because I recognized the hand of God moving. He said in His word, "And it shall come to pass afterward, that I shall pour out my spirit upon all flesh; and your sons and your daughters shall prophesy, your old men shall dream dreams, and your young men shall see visions. And also upon the servants and upon the handmaids in those days, will I pour out my spirit." [Joel 2:28,29]

So the vision God revealed was indeed a comfort to me.

The day they rolled my two sons down the hall to surgery was overwhelming. There went D. Frank, and there went Kevan. The Lord was just with me. Two of my sons at the same time was more than any mother should have to witness. The Lord was with me. It's heart-wrenching to see a mother when one child is being taken into surgery, but they were carrying two of my sons down the hall. When they brought them back, I just thanked God.

I can't describe my feeling when I found out the doctors had discovered something. At the time, I thought it was D. Frank they were talking about. I didn't know it was Kevan. I thought they meant D. Frank's kidney was getting better. We were all shocked!

This type of procedure was something new to me. When I was coming along, you didn't hear about these types of things, and I certainly never heard about anything like what the doctor found out. Now, since I've gone through this, I'd go through it again if it came to my younger children or my grandchildren. My advice to them would be go ahead, do whatever the doctors said was in their best interest. In my day, if you had kidney trouble like that, you'd die. But now, they're transplanting organs—kidneys, hearts, eyes, everything. The only thing I would hope for is that all participants involved would know the Lord.

The Lord is able to do all things. I always said the Lord is my light and my salvation. Who should I fear? That is one of my favorite scriptures. God was the first physician. He performed the first surgery on Adam. If you've got God in your life, you don't have to worry. When you're going through things, just give it to Him and it will be done right.

The Early Years

Reverend Donald Frank Waiters

Part I

I had a very humble beginning like most did. I am the fourth child, the second son of the eleven children born to Carrie Lee and Harry Lee Waiters. I was born on a Tuesday morning at two o'clock on December 30, 1947. Everyone calls me D. Frank.

My momma said I was so big, I weighed in at thirteen-and-a-half pounds or better. They told me when they put me on the scales to weigh me, I fell off. But you know what, it's not how you start—it's how you finish. I was born and raised in Heath Springs, South Carolina, where I spent the first seventeen years of my life on a farm. We were dairy farmers, cotton farmers, corn farmers, wood farmers, hog farmers—you name it, we did it on the farm. I grew up in the early '50s during my childhood days. For family outings, we used to go to the movies. Every Saturday, my mom would take us to the movies, and we would see the Westerns. I guess that's why I am hooked on Westerns today.

At the age of five, I walked to school. Buses were not in our community. Later, as times began to change, we started riding the bus; but while I attended Mount Carmel School in the country, we didn't have buses. Getting to ride the school bus was a blessing to us. For one thing, we didn't have to walk anymore; furthermore, we didn't have to worry about being called names and jeered at and made fun of while we walked to school.

When I was about seven years old, my brother Larry was born, and then there were seven of us. My daddy said that it was getting a little expensive to take seven children and my mom to the movie house, so he bought a TV. It was a combination stereo and television. We bought that back in 1954. We were the first in our neighborhood with a television. All the children in the neighborhood would come to our house to watch television. It wasn't a very big screen, but it was television. I can remember "Howdy Doody" and "Arthur Godfrey" and the "Smith Brothers." Also, Jack Parker, who brought wrestling to Charlotte, North Carolina.

The time came when our little country school was closed. While they were trying to get another school together, we went to a school named Oakridge, and then we were bused to another school, named Hillside.

I went to Mount Carmel Elementary School and then to Hillside Elementary School, and then to Hillside High School. I was just a little fellow, but I remember those cold mornings. I also remember a lady we called Mrs. Mary. She was another set of eyes in the community to help look out for the children. She would meet us at the door and put beef fat on our hands. Some call it lard, but it was warm, and it made our hands feel a whole lot better on those cold mornings. Thank God for Mrs. Mary. She was an elder who helped instill responsibility in us.

Everyone had chores to do on a daily basis. When we got home from school, there were things to be done, and that was that. We each had our own job to do, and we simply had to get the jobs done. My specific jobs were feeding the hogs and milking the cows.

Having chores to do was sometimes a chore itself, because our house was the neighborhood house. Kids who were mine and my brothers' ages would come to the house, and my mother never turned any of the children away, but we had chores to do. Our mother was everybody's mother.

I was plowing in the field at the age of seven. We had two mules—George and Lad. Then, we got a horse named Marge. My brother Ernest and I would plow, and my brother Joe would ride the mule and guide me as I plowed. Then, when we got another mule, Joe was able to plow. We were farmers, indeed. We raised cattle and hogs and we ate off the land. We grew our own things. We made our own flour, made our own meal, our own molasses, and grew potatoes and peanuts. We pretty much ate out of the garden in the summertime. We ate from our own resources. My father worked every day at one of the Springs Industries plants called Grace Bleachery.

I can remember my father working first shift, and I remember him going to second and third shift. In the early and middle '50s, when my father worked first and second shift, we were out in the fields, farming. My father was paying my grandfather to tell us what to do, and whatever he said, that's what we did.

My brothers and I worked for my dad when we were teenagers. He sent us out as plow hands. We used to go and plow for other farmers in the community. One job we had was with a gentleman name Mr. Catoe. He told my dad he had one son, and the rest were girls, and he really needed help. He asked my dad if he could hire us out, and my dad said yes.

The following morning, my dad drove us over to Mr. Catoe's farm. He had white mules, and when we went out to look at his field that needed plowing, the rows were very long. My brother and I got started. We began early that morning. When it came time for lunch, his wife came out and tried to get us to eat something, but we were taught not to eat at anyone's house—we always ate at home—so we didn't eat.

When Mr. Catoe got home that evening and saw the condition of those mules, he was infuriated.

He told my dad, "Those boys were trying to kill my mules," but all we were doing was working. We worked those mules. If they never got worked again, we worked those rascals that day. Mr. Catoe told my dad, "Don't send them boys back again. They tried to kill my mules."

Of course, we didn't go back to work for him. We worked for others. We picked cotton. We worked as a family unit in everything. We didn't work just to be working. Working as a family unit, we accomplished many things. I thank God for that.

LET THE LITTLE FELLOW SING

I remember being young and having a love for singing. I loved singing more than anything else I did. It was a way out for me. I still enjoy singing. I can always hum a tune when things are going well, and even if things are not going so well. I didn't know where singing would take me in life, but I can remember at the age of four, there was an elderly guy named Jim Tillman.

Jim pretty much didn't talk to people, so the Lord sent me out to his house to sing to him. I remember this well, because we were told to stay away from him. Everybody said Jim acted crazy, but he didn't act crazy with us. He let us come in, and we sang to him. It was four of my female cousins and me. I was the only boy. We all sang for Jim. As we got older, we still sang together. Even today, we are still together. We are blessed.

The Lord saw something in us back then. We sang to Jim that day, and within a few months, he had gone home to be with the Lord. I guess I started way back then trying to win people for the Lord.

When I was about eight years old, I sang quartet with my oldest brother Ernest and some of his friends. The other guys were older than my brother, and I was the youngest. This was in 1956. We went around to churches in the area and to different programs in and around North and South Carolina.

People would always say, "Let the little fellow sing."

That's what I did. I also sang in the choir with my dad. Singing is a part of my life; it has stayed with me through some of the rough times. Whenever I was sad, singing was how I made it through.

Growing up, we always had opportunities to sing in church. My father was the Sunday school superintendent. Whenever there was a program, he would always put our names down to sing. Since there were so many of us, the first one would sing, and we would all have to sing with that one. The second one would sing, and we would all have to sing, and so on. It was like that until we got down to Larry, Denise, and Kevan. They didn't travel and go to the different churches like we did, but we did all sing together some time.

My father believed in taking his family to church. We didn't get dropped off as some would. On Sundays after church, families didn't rush to get back to their homes. They visited with one another. I got the impression on more than one occasion they didn't want to leave. Sunday was our family together time, and we spent a lot of time in church. My mom and her sisters and brothers would talk and talk and so would a lot of other church and family members. Yes, it was quite different then. But that's the way our family did it.

As we got older we got away from doing some things. The things that were instilled as a child were still there; we just got away from them.

The scripture says in Proverbs 22:6, "Train up a child in the way he should go, and when he is old, he will not depart from it." KJV

I am here to say we were reared by the best. My mom and dad did an outstanding job with my brothers and sisters and myself. I have no regrets. My parents get two thumbs up!

Growing older, I am finding out some things. One thing I found out is love is sometimes better than money. Love for one another will enable you to accomplish many things. You can always use a little help from your friends. Two can accomplish a lot more than one in most situations. I am truly thankful my mom and dad taught us to love one another. My dad gave me words to live by: Treat others as you want to be treated.

* *

We were a close-knit family. We fought like cats and dogs, but if you said anything about one of us, another one would jump on you. We protected and watched out for each other.

When I was about ten years old, my father got me a bull. I named him Lewis. I raised this bull from a calf while he had to suck a bottle. I raised him until he became a full-grown bull. He was my family pet until I left to go to college. We began to think of Lewis as the beginning of the family fortune. He was like a part of us.

In December 1957, one of the most dramatic things in my life happened. My grandfather, my mother's father, Willie Frank Moses, died. I was named after him. For the first time in my life, I cried over the death of someone close to me.

After my grandfather died, we would go every Christmas to my grandmother's house. As a tradition, the men would go squirrel hunting. After my grandfather died, my mother and her brother, my uncle R.B., got closer. He would come to my mother's house and eat once a week.

On Christmas morning of 1958, my uncle, R.B. came over. My uncle had boys my age, and he was teaching them to hunt. I wanted to go hunting with them, but my momma told me, "Don't go."

I was just pleading with my momma to let me go, but she said, "No, I don't want you to go. Something doesn't feel right."

I asked my uncle to talk to my momma, so he talked her into letting me go with him hunting. The deal was that I couldn't just wander off—I had to follow him wherever he went, and I did. You wouldn't believe it—we were in the woods, and I got shot in the leg.

We tried to hide it from my mom, but we couldn't. She knew something had happened, and she was very upset. My dad cried because I got shot. He carried me around like a fool. I couldn't walk for a while. Even to this day, I have some of those pellets in me.

I often think about things that my momma said. She could see things happening before they happened. She may not tell you what she saw, but I learned later on in life that if your mother tells you not to do something, don't do it, because there will be consequences.

My mother always had something to eat. She was a dietician. She cooked in restaurants and later with the school district. But initially she started cooking at restaurants, and we always ate well. My mother always made us fresh food. We didn't eat leftovers. We really didn't know what leftovers were, because everything was always eaten at dinnertime. We ate the best of everything. We ate what we raised and grew on the farm. My mother would also bring things home they gave her at the cafeteria.

I remember my mother didn't work on Sundays, because we had to be at church. Millers Cafeteria, my mothers employer, told her if she worked on Sundays she could take food home to her family, which worked out pretty well because we had church on the second and fourth Sunday, and my mother would work the first and third Sunday. We ate well all the time.

My father and mother made it work somehow. They didn't make a lot of money, but things just seemed to work. I don't know how other families did it, but when we were coming up, everybody worked for the house. Whatever money we made was contributed to the household. We brought everything into the house and then my father or my mother would distribute it out. That's how our family did it; that was part of our upbringing. My mother would also do things for people and never look for anything in return, so we, the children, had to adopt the same attitude. I hear my brothers and sisters say sometimes, "Our father ruined us because he made us do things and not to look for anything back."

Because we were raised that way, some people now think we ought to be like our dad. Our dad has been known to go in the hole to help people, but from what I can remember, during those times, it seemed people cared more about each other than nowadays. People had more love in their hearts. They were more concerned about your welfare. In those times, when none of us really had much, you could actually trust your neighbor and you could count on your neighbor. They would watch out for your children. This was a plus for us, because this was also the time of cross burnings. I lived through someone burning a cross in our front yard.

In my childhood days, we lived in a neighborhood where everyone knew each other. Most of them were family, and we had respect for each other. We faced some difficult times when crosses were burned in our yards, but for the most part, we were a strong neighborhood that stayed together. I see some differences now; some people don't have the love, as they should. My mother and father brought us up to love, and that's what we did.

We like to talk about how times are better now, but we have become a nation who has forgotten where we came from. We have no idea about our purpose and less of an idea of who we are. I remember a time in America when people were concerned about their neighbor, but not today. Some have adopted the idea of "me, myself, and I." Most folks don't know their neighbors—they don't even know who lives next door. How can they be concerned about someone they don't know? There is a belief we are just here to have a good time and no one can stop us. We must get back to the old adage that says, *Love thy neighbor as thyself.*

My brothers, Ernest, Joe, and I did have some time off the farm. We were in the 4-H club and showed animals, forestry, and agriculture. I can remember Mr. Robert Smith was our county agent. He would come and do little extra things for my dad and granddad. They thought the world of Mr. Smith. We also got close with his family.

What I remember most growing up on the farm was working all the time. I also sang on the school choir and played football and basketball. I had a good time growing up. I thank God for allowing me to go back in time and share some of those childhood memories with you.

As the World Turns

D. Frank

Facing the Real World

Growing up, I had five brothers and five sisters. Of course we had our sibling rivalries, but being the fourth child, I was considered one of the elders. I was already in college. The younger group, which included Kevan, was just growing up. Because of the difference in our ages, I watched them become young adults, though they were still in elementary school when I left home.

Being away from home did not take away the things my father instilled in me. He told me, and I will never forget, that everything we did involved him, and everything he did involved us. We needed to be careful how we carried ourselves among people so our name would be a name people could trust. If you gave a person your word, you kept your word. If you shook hands with that person, it was confirmed. You didn't have to have a paper signed; your word was sufficient.

My father said, "If you can't do something, don't say you can, and don't do it. Your word is all you have."

My father also told me to be conscious of what people said to me, remember what they told me, and remember what I told them. Today, years after my father told me those things, my wife now tells me, "You remember everything." That was my father's mandate—I grew up on that.

I went to Friendship College in Rock Hill, South Carolina, in 1965, straight out of high school. I was on a work-study program. I found out that when they say work, they mean work.

The president of the college told my dad, "You bring them, and we will find something for them to do to keep them."

I had two jobs at the school; it kept my mom and dad from having to send money. Any money that was made was house money—it came to the house to pay bills. It was never your money, even though you went out and earned it.

During that summer, I got my first job away from my house. I was working as an orderly for twenty-five cents an hour at a Seminary Hospital in Alexandria, Virginia. I worked that job for two days. After two days, I met a fellow that told me he had a job that would pay me twice as much.

I asked him, "What is the job?"

He said, "It's hard work."

I said, "What is hard work?"

He said, "Lifting bricks."

I asked him if it was anything like pulpwood, and he didn't know anything about pulpwood. I fell right in and the brick and mortar game was nothing like pulpwood. I worked all that summer. I made money that was mine for the first time. I had control over it. I wasn't in my daddy's house; I was staying with my aunt and uncle, and I gave them something while I was staying there for the summer.

My dad told me to come home and go back to school. I didn't want to go to school, but he insisted that I come.

He threatened me. He said, "If you don't come, I will come and get you."

My aunt told me, "You know your daddy don't play, so the best thing is to go back to school."

I went back to school. After that year, I decided that I would drop out of college and leave home. I even made the statement that I would never return. My momma told me if I dropped out, they were going to draft me. Of course, I thought I knew all of the answers.

I said, "I've got it covered."

• •

I dropped out of college, and within four months I was drafted. Before I move on with this part of the story, let me tell you right now, I was the first one of the eleven siblings to return home, and I thank God for bringing me back.

In 1966, I went to Washington, DC, and started working for Eastern Airlines. In December 1966, I got a greeting from Uncle Sam. On February 1, 1967, I was to report to Fort Bragg, North Carolina for induction into the military. I was at Fort Bragg and Fort Jackson, South Carolina. In July 1967, I went to Vietnam.

I was in Vietnam from July of '67 to February of '68. I saw quite a bit of action, about which I will not go into great detail, but believe me when I say there's no place like home.

I was able to keep my younger brother from coming to Vietnam, because the U.S. had passed a law that no two brothers could be in a combat zone at the same time. A lady in Charleston, South Carolina, had lost four sons and had one son left.

In February of 1968, I went to South Korea. I was sick—I had witnessed so much death. As if I hadn't seen enough in Vietnam, Uncle Sam sent me to Korea. I was there from February until August of 1968, serving my country.

Upon returning from Korea, my orders were to report to Fort Hood, Texas. I went to the Pentagon and asked them to change my orders, because I had been away from home since June of 1967. Sending me to Fort Hood would be like being in Vietnam; I would be away from my family. The only post that had an opening was in Fort Myers, Virginia. My MOS [Military Occupational Specialty] allowed me to go there, so I took it.

I was assigned to E Company, Honor Guard. It was a spit and polish unit. Top Dog Company. I was in a firing company. We were the unit that did the gun salutes at the gravesites for soldiers who were either killed in battle or elderly. I served from August of 1968 to January 30, 1970.

Being in Fort Myers, my coverage duty area included the White House. I spent a lot of time in the West Wing during this stint of my duty. I performed in the inauguration of President Richard Nixon in 1969 and in President Dwight Eisenhower's funeral. I was in the firing party and a commander. I served in three different companies: E Company, B Company and O Company. It was a stressful time for me. The ordeal of Vietnam took a toll on me. I was learning to deal with things—searching for inner peace and finding none. No one was listening to me.

I married Regina Foster, my first wife, on July 5, 1969, while I was stationed at Fort Myers. Our first child was born in October 1969. Her name is Jocquelyn LaChown Waiters- Reeves now. She has a son. His name is Thomas Frank Reeves. My first wife and I had some problems, but we tried to work them out.

In 1970 when it was time to re-enlist or get out, I got out. The hippies would come to town every weekend, and we would have to go to the White House and spend the whole weekend there, and I hated it with a passion. I was just tired of it.

After my tour of duty ended, I was trying to get back to life as a civilian. Little did I know, Vietnam had embedded in my soul. I was irritated and restless all the time. I moved to Philadelphia, then to New Jersey. I was in a management position, and I was never home during the week. My daughter was now in school, and she wasn't having anything but problems.

Every now and then, I had a flashback of Vietnam. This thing had crept across its boundaries into my life, wreaking havoc down to my core.

The Beatles said it best in the lyrics of a song, "*Help/I need somebody.*"

I was doing all this moving because I didn't understand all the things that were happening to me. I had gone through some experiences in Vietnam, and I wasn't talking about them. Maybe it would have helped if I had gone through some debriefing or something, but there was nothing I knew of that would help me better understand what was happening. I would go to the VA hospitals complaining about conditions. They would tell me there was no way for this to be happening, but this was real—no place to run, no place to hide, trapped in my own skin.

I was working for Eastern Airlines at the time, and I had to leave that job because of the situation I was in. I thought changing jobs so I could be home would help, so I resigned in 1976. I got a job at *The Washington Post* in '76 or '77 printing newspapers. There had been a strike, and they were hiring replacements. When I went for an interview I met Donald Graham. We found out both of us had served in A Company, Second of the Fifth Calvary, but at different times. I don't think that's what got me hired, but I got hired.

After about four years at *The Post*, I had to leave that job for the same reason I had left the one at Eastern. Again, I was trying to deal with stress and all the other things that came with my situation. Problems got worse.

During this time, my wife inevitably left me. It was December 19, 1978. I went to work that morning, and when I came home from work, my house was cleaned out. Nothing was there. All of our furniture was gone—everything. All I was left with were my clothes. Those times were hard. She wouldn't let me see our daughter. She was angry with me, and I was angry with her. She wanted a divorce, and I didn't, but I wanted access to my daughter, so I gave her the divorce. The judge granted me custody of our daughter. We got a divorce in 1980. I moved back to South Carolina and lived with my mom and dad, until my father passed away in 1983. With leaving college, getting drafted, living in Washington, DC, my stint in the army, getting married, having my first child, getting divorced, and moving back to South Carolina, I was really facing the real world.

I was looking for something I could not find, and I used many things that I thought would relieve me or give me peace, but I found none. The drugs, alcohol, and women—I needed peace.

In 1980, I was in contact with my brother Kevan again on a regular basis because he was stationed at Parris Island, in South Carolina, as a drill instructor. I was staying in Lancaster. I would go down and spend weekends with him. We did different things. We were partners in selling life insurance.

We had a good relationship. We started a business, South Falk Unlimited, plus we had the family business, Uncle Buds. We sold insurance, made trips—we took people to funerals, on vacations, family reunions, and stuff like that, and I had my daughter with me.

Kevan met and married his wife in 1982, and I met and married my second wife, Sandra Jean, in 1984. I had a son from this marriage. My daughter was fourteen years old at the time and didn't like me getting married, so she left me and went to stay with her mom. My wife Sandra and I moved to California, and she got pregnant with my son. We had been out there for two years, and issues started coming up—things that I couldn't deal with.

My family was planning a memorial service for my dad along with a family reunion, and they asked if I was coming. I made preparations to come home, and my wife didn't want to come. She had somehow made it up in her mind I was bringing her to South Carolina to leave her. I told her I wasn't going to do that, but she insisted I was.

She kept saying, "You're going to leave me."

I kept telling her, "No, I am not."

All she knew was I would be better off without her. She began making the statement, "You will be better off without me." She started walking out in traffic and I would have to pull her back.

We came home as planned, but while we were there in South Carolina, her frustrations got the best of her; she killed herself. I had a one-year-old son to care for. My life was up in the air, but my son needed me. He became my something to live for. My brother went from active duty to reserve status, then back to active duty. All during this time, we stayed in contact with each other, doing things with each other.

We'd done so many things together, and then I was called to preach. I accepted the call in 1982.

Kevan and I had been on a trip to Nashville, and we were coming back. Just outside of Atlanta, while he and I were talking, the Holy Spirit was moving in the car, and finally I broke down and told my brother I had been called to preach.

He said, "Whew! Thank God it's you and it's not me! I knew He was after somebody!"

That was February 1, 1982, and I didn't do anything. I told my pastor. He told me I had to tell the people. I told him I wasn't going to tell anybody!

In 1987, the Lord sent me a third wife, Nita Michelle Johnson, who I married in 1988. We were married six weeks after I met her, and we've been married ever since. She helped me raise my son from three years old, and now he's grown and married.

Nita and I lived in Washington all the time we've been married. We moved to South Carolina in 2005 to pursue other avenues the Lord placed in our hearts.

Nita was sent by God. We have been married eighteen years. The Lord told me He would send me a wife. He told me that her name would be Johnson. At the time, I was serving as a pastor, and there were two Johnson ladies at my church. I thought the Lord meant one of them, but He didn't. I had not met my wife when He told me this. I met her for the first time in October of 1987. I didn't know how old she was, but I knew she talked a lot. I said to myself, *She talks too much.* I didn't want to see her again.

The Lord told me, "Don't look at the outer appearance, but at the heart." She was kind of large, about 260 lbs. Looking at her today, that wife who was 260 pounds is now 142 pounds. I am so thankful to God; He gave me a beautiful relationship when He sent her my way.

We too have had some rough times, but through it all, we've made it. She has been an inspiration to me, and I have been an inspiration to her. God kept us together, and He made us whole. We have been faithful to God first and also to each other. I don't know how I would have made it if she had not been the woman she is. She was nineteen years old when I met her. I really didn't know how old she was, but God told me to marry her. Out of obedience, I married her, and that was one of the best things I could have done.

She keeps me grounded in what I am called of God to do. When we got reacquainted, I said to her, "I know this is going to sound crazy, but will you marry me? The Lord told me to marry you, and I want to know, will you marry me?"

She said, "Yeah."

I told her up front I wasn't in love with her, but I was being obedient to God in asking her.

I don't know for what she had been asking the Lord. I just knew I had so many shortcomings, and I wanted God's will for my life. Some people thought the reason we married was that she was pregnant, but none of that happened, and none of what was being said was true. I just know there are benefits in obeying the voice of God.

After nineteen years of marriage, I love my wife so much today. We have come through adversity, but our bond has only been strengthened. I have had a stroke, blindness, and kidney disease. She has epileptic seizures and has had brain surgery. The Lord has blessed us to be husband and wife, mother and father, pastor and his lady.

THE FIFTH SON

KEVAN LAFAYETTE WAITERS

I am truly blessed to be alive today. I was told the hardest pregnancy my mother had was when she carried me. There was talk like I almost didn't make it here.

I would say my childhood was very unique. I was born and grew up during the late fifties and sixties and the Vietnam War. My father kept our family thriving as best he could. My great-grandfather, Can Waiters, purchased 200 acres of land. His desire was, "As long as there is a Waiters living, they will always have a place to stay." My father worked and reared his family off of the land.

In December 1957, the same year I was born, my grandfather—my mother's father—passed away. His name was Willie Frank. Even though I never got the chance to really meet my grandfather, my grandmother was there, whom I loved very dearly. My mother told me that she and three of her seven sisters were pregnant and had miscarriages when my grandfather passed away. I was about five months old at the time, and my mother was embarrassed to tell her sisters she was pregnant again, because she already had nine children, but my grandmother had eleven children, and my great-grandmother had eleven children. Sounds like a family tradition.

When I was three years old, my father was 38. He worked for Springs Industries, the major employer of the area, which at the time was one of the largest cotton manufacturers. He was determined to take care of his family, and he did that very well. He worked the cotton field in the morning and worked the cotton mill in the evening.

We raised a lot of cotton. Between the first and sixth grade, I can remember picking cotton. If we picked enough cotton, we could pay for our way to go to the county fair in October. The number of bales of cotton we picked determined how much we got paid. My mother would go out into the fields and pick cotton right along with us. She always picked twice the cotton we picked.

COTTON DAYS WITH GEORGE AND DELLA

Cotton was usually harvested in September and early October. Today, there are big tractors, but when my brothers were plowing, we didn't have that luxury. We had two mules: George and Della.

There was a lot to do with cotton when we planted it. The field required a lot of work; the dirt was almost like powder. We made these really nice rows in it, then dragged a log across it and made it flat. We used a cotton planter. The cotton planter did three things: opened the furrows, planted the seeds, and then it covered them up. Next, we had to chop the cotton out. Because of the nutrients in the soil, we did a lot of weeding so the weeds wouldn't get all the nutrients, and the stalks would have a chance to thrive. We also weeded out some of the stalks to get a stronger stalk. We sometimes killed two plants to save one. There's a lot of work to cotton. Then, we had to use DDT and different chemicals to keep the boll weevils from taking the cotton. As we plowed the cotton, we had to treat it so nothing would eat the cotton. We had to have a really good grade of cotton when we were getting ready to put it on the market.

When I was working in those fields, I'd wear a hat and long sleeves. The key to keeping cool in the field is not short sleeves or tank tops. In actuality, if you wanted to be cool, you stopped the sun's rays from beaming directly onto your skin. We were cooler with long sleeves than with short sleeves. And the straw hat would help block the sun beaming down.

We would take a break at lunchtime, when it was really hot, and we'd watch *All My Children* and *General Hospital* on TV. Once that was over, before *The Edge of Night* would come on, we'd have to go back out into the fields and work until it got dark. Cotton was a very hard job. Once we finished picking our fields, we would go and help others who had big fields and needed assistance.

George and Della were almost like a part of the family, because they did a lot of the work. We didn't have any tractors, so those mules plowed everything. The rule of the house was every-body—man, woman, boy, girl, or mule had to pull their load.

Harder Than Picking Cotton

I met an elderly lady in Florida years later. She asked, "What is harder than picking cotton?"

I was trying to think because cotton is pretty tough. I said, "I don't know. You've got me stumped. What is harder than picking cotton?"

She said, "Chopping cotton."

She was about right, because chopping cotton was pretty hard too.

My other grandfather and grandmother, Henry and Bessie Waiters, had a significant hand in my upbringing. I was close to being ten years old when Henry passed away in 1966. He never would let us play around; he always looked for something for us to do.

This meant I also had my time on the farm. We grew various types of products. We grew sweet potatoes, corn, watermelons, cantaloupes, cucumbers, tomatoes, cabbages, greens, green beans, peas, carrots, squash and beets. I can remember there was a cherry tree between my grandfather's house and our home, and my grandmother didn't want us to go in the cherry tree. We would try to sneak and get cherries when she wasn't looking. Those were some of the best cherries; it was the only tree in the middle of the field.

I'd see my brothers plowing. I didn't know it at the time, but I was supposed to be watching everything they did. I was supposed to be learning the plowing terminology, so that when I came of age to plow, if my father said, "I need you to go do this," or, "I need you to plow," or put down fertilizer or put seeds in there, I would know what to do.

I was supposed to be paying attention to what my brothers were doing; what type of plows they used, the terminology: what they would call "laying it by," "rolling the millers," or "putting the fir in." Those are plowing terminologies. I had to learn what those meant, because when my father said, "I want you to go roll a miller in the corn," he wasn't going to take me down there and show me what to do.

My dad taught us all at a very early age. That was farm living, and I was supposed to be paying attention. When it was time for me to take over that job, I had to know what to do. Learning how to plow, and things of that nature, was a profession, and it was a trade we had to learn.

My father raised hogs all my life. I can't ever remember hogs not being on our property.

I remember one time, this was after I had grown up, done my stint in the military, and moved back home, that I sold all the hogs. When my mother found out I had done that, she called me and said, "You better get those hogs back before sundown. There have always been hogs on this property, and there always will be."

I guess you know what I did. I put my rear end in high gear and went out and bought some hogs before sundown.

We did a community event where everybody would get together, and we would kill hogs on our property. We'd put this big barrel out there, fill it with water, and put a fire under it so the water would come to a boil. Someone would take the rifle and shoot the hog and we'd cut his throat. We'd put the hog in the barrel of boiling water, and then we would hang him up. Then, we would start an assembly line. One guy would be cutting the hog and another one would be chopping him up. You'd take the hams and hang and cure them. You'd take the pork chops, the tenderloin, and the bacon and cure the meat that needed to be cured.

We had a smokehouse, where we would hang the meat, salt it down, put a sack over it, and put molasses around it. It made the ham really sweet when we cooked it.

We did that, plus we'd kill our own bulls. We rarely ever killed any cows, but we'd kill the bulls. We would take the hide and stretch it—we'd use everything. Every product from the animal that we could use, we used it.

CREAM, BUTTER, MILK, AND MOLASSES

We had milk cows. We also had beef cows, but we had milk cows because we sold milk. We also made barrels and barrels of molasses and would sell it to the public. We had to provide for the family any way we could. Milk and molasses were two of the major products we sold to the community. People would come from all around and buy milk and molasses.

We also made butter. The milk was put in a churn. It was almost like making ice cream. We'd keep churning the milk and churning the milk, and then it would make butter. In order to make really good butter, you have to have cream, so we'd milk the cows early in the morning and you would get a really good cream. We kept the cows bred so they kept producing milk. You ever milked a cow in the morning before you went to school? It left an awful smell on your hands.

CAUGHT IN THE MIDDLE

They decided to integrate some of the schools in Lancaster County, but not all of them. They sent us a letter telling all the children who lived in my community that we'd be going to South Middle School. Leaving everyone and everything I knew, going to a different environment. We were going to be caught in the middle of this transition. The whites didn't know us. And there was a rivalry going on between blacks from other neighborhood schools.

I said, "South Middle School?"

We had never heard of South Middle School. We had been going to Hillside all of our lives, and we didn't know anything about South Middle School.

When I got to South, it was my siblings, the students from our community, and a few other people, and we were the only blacks in the school. Things were very different from Hillside. I had been in a school where I was in the choir and in the drama club. I was involved in a lot of things, had a lot of friends, and went different places.

These kids had to get used to me, and I had to get used to them. I had gone to a whole different environment and had to adjust to the integration scenario.

We really didn't have a problem with it, because we were already taught that you treat people the way you want to be treated. I was able to meet some new friends. Once I got in there and settled in, things worked out okay.

I asked my father if I could play sports. He said I could pick one sport, and I could play sports for one year, so I chose football and played as a wide receiver for South. I thought I was pretty good.

From '70 to '71, all of the schools had to be integrated. I brought a note home for my father to sign me up to play again the next year, and he said, "No. I told you that you could play for one year."

I said, "I thought you were joking. I think I'm pretty good, and the coaches think I'm pretty good."

He said, "You need to find a job."

At that time, we were in the heart of the Vietnam War. My brother Ernest had graduated from college and got drafted. My brother D. Frank was in college and got drafted. My brother Joe dropped out of college and got drafted. It was pretty tough. It was a crucial time in the family where anything I could do to support the family financially, I needed to do that.

One of my first jobs was at South Middle School, washing dishes in the cafeteria. When the other kids were at lunch and playing around, I spent my lunch break washing dishes for a quarter an hour. I was getting probably an hour a day—maybe five dollars a month. Back then, at twelve years old, five dollars a month was pretty good.

Fights were occurring everyday. My siblings and friends were glad to get out of school and back to the safe haven of our own neighborhoods. In our own yard where we could relax and let our hair down and just be boys.

Our lawn was about three acres. The front yard was a perfect football field. My mother had flowers growing along the sidewalks in front of the house, and she had these little metal rails that you could stick down for decoration around the flowerbed. My father told us not to be playing in the front yard, but we were out there playing anyway. My brother Larry was running down the sideline close to the house. I was determined to tackle him and not let him get by me. Larry was pretty quick, and when I grabbed hold of him, he slung me off, and I slid into the flowerbed rails. One caught my foot and sliced it open. We took off my shoe, and my foot was bleeding pretty badly.

We said we couldn't tell anyone what happened because we'd get a whipping, so Larry got some baby powder and Vaseline, and we doctored it up and wrapped it. Each day, my foot was getting sorer because it was getting infected. It got to the point I could hardly walk on it. My sister Janice and her husband Larry Dixon were living with us at the time. Larry asked me what was wrong.

I said, "I want to show you something."

I pulled my sock down and showed him, and he said, "I'm telling Mother." He told my mother, and she took me to the doctor.

It was too late to sew it up, but it was a pretty bad gash. It should have been sewn up when it first happened, but it wasn't, and it got infected. I had been putting powder on it.

The doctor looked at it and said, "Well, who did *this* to it? Who did *that* to it? You actually saved your foot. I'm going to give you some antibiotics."

He said I'd probably never be able to wear a boot. Worst of all, I had to wear a bedroom shoe to school, and that wasn't too cool. Later on, when I went into service and I had to wear a boot, I never had a problem with it. I kept expecting it to swell to the point where it would be hard to wear a boot, but it healed up perfectly, and I never had a problem with it. The Lord had to be preserving me for something, because I sure had my share of bumps, cuts, and bruises coming up.

My father had a pond dug on our property; one day, one of my brother's friends was ice-skating on the pond, and he fell in and drowned. After that, we were banned from going swimming. I didn't learn to swim until I went into service because we couldn't go to the pond by ourselves. We used to try to sneak down there and swim, but I still didn't learn to swim until I went into the Marine Corps.

* *

I settled in pretty well at this school, but I still felt like I lost a lot of my friends going to South Middle School. One time, I spent the night with a friend, Larry Truesdale. He spent the night at my house, but I had never spent the night at his. I went over, and Larry's mother cooked dinner.

We drank a lot of milk, but we drank it out of metal cups. We didn't like to drink milk from a glass, and I didn't like buttermilk. I didn't drink it.

Well, I was raised to never disrespect anyone and always eat whatever was put on my plate. At dinner, Larry's mother fixed us these tall glasses of buttermilk—in a glass. I thought, *Oh no what am I going to do?* I had been taught to respect my elders. There was only one thing I could think to do—I just closed my eyes and killed it.

His mother said, "Are you done with that? You want some more?"

I said, "No ma'am, no ma'am." I didn't want to tell her I didn't even drink buttermilk—especially in a glass!

We played intramural sports on weekends, basketball and things like that, but mainly we had a lot of work to do around the farm. Growing up, we took calves to the fair to try to win a blue ribbon. Every spring the cows would have calves. We'd each pick one out, and our job was to train that calf. We'd train all spring and all summer for the county fair. My father would buy a little halter for them. We'd teach them how to move and how to hold their heads up.

My family had won numerous blue ribbons, and I wanted to keep the tradition going. If a calf won a blue ribbon at the county fair, the calf went to the state fair. When other kids were playing around, I had to be home training my calf. I didn't have time to be playing and messing around. I had chores to do, and I had to train my calf. The more time I put in with my calf, the better my calf would be when I got ready to take him to the fair.

My brother Larry and I joined the 4-H club. They provided us with one hundred biddies, maybe a day or two old. My father had a pen built, and we had these lights on them until they were big enough to survive on their own. We would pick the roosters out of there and keep them in separate pens. Later on, we would kill the roosters for food and use the chickens to lay eggs.

The 4-H club required us to bring twelve of them to the fair. If the chickens won a ribbon, they would auction them off, and we got to keep the money. The chickens that lived, we could keep, but we had to present twelve at the fair. Our chickens were winning lots of blue ribbons, so we had the chickens and the calves.

We actually had some time when we didn't do anything. When we wanted to sit back and watch a good Western. Larry, Denise, and I would go out into the garden and get some corn to make popcorn. It grows just like regular corn. We picked it, shucked it, and shelled it off the ear. Then, we would put it in the pan and make some popcorn.

I would say my childhood was very rewarding. I had a lot of things that kept me busy.

Midnight and Sweepstakes

When I was young, I wanted a pony. I wanted a pony really badly. We had the mules, and we used them to work and plow, but I wanted my own pony.

My baby brother, Harry, talked Daddy into buying him a pony—Harry could talk Daddy into doing almost anything. We named the pony Midnight.

Midnight was perfect for me, but Harry was too small. My dad bought him for Harry, but actually Midnight was mine. I'd ride Midnight everywhere and do different things with him. We later bought another pony about Midnight's size named Sweepstakes, who had four or five colts. We ended up with a little horse ranch with Midnight and Sweepstakes.

We had a black horse named Marge. I never did get a chance to ride Marge. My brother Ernest would race Marge with my cousins' horse, named Blackie. Marge died when I was really small.

No Shame on the Name

I went to Hillside Elementary School and Hillside High School. Schools were still segregated then—black and white schools. We went to Hillside, which had the elementary and high schools— all twelve grades—there.

I remember my first-grade teacher, Miss Bradley. Going into the first grade, I was excited about everything. My brothers and sister had been to the school, so my name—the Waiters name— was very prominent in the school. My brothers, Ernest and D. Frank, played football.

They all got jobs driving school buses, and Mom didn't want Joe driving a school bus, either, because she thought he was a little too small. My brothers and sisters laid a very tough foundation, which I had to carry on without bringing any shame on the Waiters name.

Our principal was named Mr. Nichols, and he was one of the tough characters. He was a real stocky guy. Anything we did out of line, he knew my parents, and they found out. If we had to get paddled at school, we got another one when we got home because we embarrassed the Waiters name.

At our school, we got a lot of books that were old, but we'd get a new book cover to put on the book. If we ever tore up book cover, we could just get some brown paper and tape it down. We very rarely got new books. Sometimes, the books would have new covers on them, but the pages inside the book were still old. We'd put a book cover over the book and it would make it look like we had a new book. When I was in the fifth or sixth grade, we started getting some new books.

I can remember Miss Bradley, a very nice person. She really got me started academically. I read a lot and learned to enjoy school. I was involved in a lot of activities in school from the first to the sixth grade. During that time, I was on the honor roll, in the drama club—just about every activity I could do, I was involved in it.

We Grew Up In Church

In 1865, my great-grandfather, Can Waiters, founded our church, New Hope Baptist Church. One of the things my father always did, which I try to instill in my family, is every Sunday morning, we'd get up and have family prayer. I didn't know this at the time, but when my father was praying, I really didn't understand it. He would always say he wanted to send a special blessing out to the bereaved family.

Well, one of our aunts had married into the Reid family, and I thought he was talking about the Reids, but he was talking about people—everyone who'd had a death in their family. It took me until later to understand what he meant.

My father was a very religious person. He was definitely, without a doubt, a Christian. He was the superintendent of our church for over thirty years. When we went to Sunday school, even if no one else was at church, we were.

My mother was the church secretary for about thirty years. With my mother as the secretary and my father as the superintendent, our family grew up in the church. We worked hard six days a week, but on Sunday, the whole family went to church. I can remember our church was an old, white church, and we used to have to light the gas heaters in the winter so when other families came in for Sunday school, it would be warm.

Because we were in different age brackets, there was a different Sunday school class for each of us. As we grew older, I began teaching Sunday school and working in the church. Teaching Sunday school was a very rewarding experience for me because it made me study. With my father being superintendent, we didn't get away with anything. We had to remember what we read and be able to talk about the Sunday school lesson. We could be called on at any time.

Because my mother was secretary of the church, anytime we had a holiday—Mother's Day, Father's Day, or Easter—we had to give a speech or sing a song. My mother automatically put our names on the roster, so we knew we were going to have to go up in front of the church and sing or give a speech. Some kids would go up there and say, "Easter egg, Easter egg, don't you cry/I'm going to eat you by and by." They had some little, simple stuff like that, and everybody would laugh.

We would get up—we could do stuff in a group—and we'd have to sing. We'd say, "I'm going to call my brother up to help me sing," and when he got up there, he'd say, "I'm going to call my brother up," or, "I'm going to call my sister up to help me." We ended up singing about three different songs, so we had to make sure you learned them.

Looking back, when I was in high school and was given the option to take a written or oral test, I'd choose oral. A lot of people are afraid to get up in front of groups and say anything, but I had been doing it all my life in church. That's a good foundation for children. Churches don't do that a lot today, but it's very rewarding, it's fun, and you have a good time. It is something I hope people will keep doing, and I hope that the churches won't get so commercial or political that they leave the little kids out.

We had church service every other Sunday. We'd hang around after church when Rev. Jones would preach, and he would give us a quarter. We'd take that quarter, and my father would stop by the store and let us spend it. That was a big thing for me, Larry, and Denise when we were growing up.

My father helped the Cement and Gum Construction Company out of Ohio by doing some work in this area in the late forties. He was helping to build Grace Bleachery, a subsidiary of Springs Industries. When that project was completed, the construction company wanted my father to go with them other places and help them with other buildings and structures.

My father said no, he had to stay and raise his family. He would only work up until harvest time with them, and then he worked his own business of raising his family and his farm.

In 1950, my father started working at the Grace Bleachery on a permanent basis. Ten years passed, and when I was three years old, his hand got caught in a machine, and it cut three of his fingers off. The small finger's the only one that didn't get cut from the joint area. I can remember they brought the fingers home, put them in a cloth, and put them in a drawer.

I was curious; I wanted to see those fingers. So while no one was looking, I went in there and looked. Today, at age fifty, I can still remember. I can remember seeing those fingers wrapped up in a white handkerchief. That was pretty rough for a three-year-old to see. Many times, I wish I hadn't gone in there. No one else knew I had gone in there, and that was terrorizing for a little guy. I guess at the time, there wasn't medical technology to sew them back on, so my father lost the tips of those three fingers. It never stopped him or dampened his spirit. He was one of the nicest people you'd ever want to meet. I can't ever remember him being upset. I never heard my father curse or saw him drink alcohol or anything of that nature. I never heard my father say anything out of line to anyone. In fact, I used to wonder why he wouldn't get upset. I was very proud of my dad; I wanted to be just like him.

My father was like a jack-of-all-trades, and he mastered quite a few of them. He shoed horses, he could work on cars, and he laid bricks. After his fingers got cut, it limited some of the things he could do, but it didn't change his attitude. It didn't change him, nor did it change the way he carried and conducted himself; those things were the same.

Guys would come from all around to my dad's shop, directly across from my grandparents' home. People would bring their horses, and my father would shoe them. This was exciting to me, because I saw a lot of Western movies where they show the blacksmith making the coals hot and making the shoes. My father used to do that. I thought my dad was pretty cool. I thought about trying to pick up that trade, but I never followed through with it. He used to do a lot of different things to help in the community.

The number "3" really played a significant part in my life. As you will continue to see throughout the story how this number keeps popping up.

I was three years old and my father had three fingers cut off. My mother had children in groups of three, and there are more threes to come.

My mother was always a very good cook. She worked in the school cafeteria at McDonald Green Elementary School and in the Rice building. She worked at Miller's-Cafeteria on Main Street. To me, my mother was like a professional cook. She could prepare a menu that was out of this world.

After prayer, we'd sit down and have breakfast, and then we'd go to church. One thing about eating at our family's kitchen table—whenever you ate, you had to eat what you put on your plate. You could never leave anything on your plate. We used to argue about biscuits. My mother used to cook a lot of biscuits to eat with our molasses.

Another thing we couldn't do when we sat down for dinner, or any meal, was, claim things. If there were only four biscuits left on the plate, and you weren't through eating what was on your plate, you couldn't say, "That biscuit's mine." You had to eat what was on your plate first. My parents had some pretty strict rules we had to live by, and there wasn't any such thing as a microwave or anything like that.

Once dinner was served, and the food was put on the table, you didn't come back later on and cook something. That was a definite no.

One of my favorite cakes is an Italian cheesecake. Every year, for as long as I can remember, if I am in town, my mother makes that for my birthday and sings happy birthday to me. I love my momma. I still look forward to that today, and my mother is 86 years old.

My mother and father were 18 and 19 when they got married and started their family. I think they did a really good job at raising us. I probably spent more time with my mother, because she didn't work when I was born. I was a difficult pregnancy for my mother, and I'm the only one she doesn't remember giving birth to.

She said she had to ask the nurse if I had both hands and all of my fingers and toes.

The nurse asked, "You haven't seen your baby?"

She said, 'No."

The nurse got me and brought me in to my mother. Mom said I had sandy brown—almost red—hair and dark skin. Denise and I are the only two that have the darker complexions in the family. My brothers told us we weren't my parents' and that they gave them the wrong baby in the hospital.

All eleven children in my family attended college. Some completed college, and some didn't, but every one of us went to a college. Just to be able to do that alone with all of the turmoil my parents faced—going through the Depression—is a great accomplishment for my parents.

My mother says they came to draft my father in World War II, and he was out plowing in the fields. He told them he was providing for his family, so they decided not to draft him and let him stay back. He was taking care of his father, his mother, and my mother, and let's not forget about the children that God had given them. They had just had a baby, so he didn't get drafted into the military.

Another lesson I learned from my father growing up was how to save. My father built his own home. He used the timber off the property. They put a sawmill on the land, cut the timber, and built his house. As his family grew, he added on.

We were one of the first families in that area to have a split-level home. We had two bedrooms and a bath upstairs and several bedrooms and a bath downstairs. With a big family, he ended up building a pretty good sized home, and he never had a mortgage. That was pretty smart of him.

We were one of the first families to get a color television. Before the color televisions came out, they had this film you could buy, and it had red, yellow, and blue stripes in it. When people would walk into the red part, they'd be red, and when they walked into the blue part, they'd be blue. That was about the closest you would come to a color TV. People would come down, and they wouldn't want to go home at night; we'd have to run them home.

We were also one of the first families to get a phone. It was on a party line, which meant there were two or three people on that line. My aunt next door and another lady down the street were on that line. Growing up, a lot of times we'd have to wait to use the phone. My sister, Denise, would eavesdrop on my aunt. The next day, she'd be talking to our mother and telling her what was going on, and our mother would ask, "Where did you get all of this from?"

Before we had gas and electrical stoves, I can remember my brothers and I had to cut wood, because that was how the heating and cooking was done. We used to haul and sell a lot of wood to people in the county. I used to look up to my father; he would help out the elderly and the widows, the sick and the shut-ins. Those were a lot of things he'd cover in his prayers on Sunday mornings. I gained respect for my dad early on in life; in my eyes, he was a Christian.

I remember once, there was snow on the ground, and we were all settled in.

This lady called and said, "Harry, I don't have a stick of wood on the ground."

We had to go out and cut wood, not only for her, but for other people, too. My father knew that lady wouldn't be able to pay us. My brothers and I were upset because we were already settled into our warm house, and we had to go cut the wood for her and others and carry it to them. Sometimes we got compensated, and other times we didn't.

My grandmother had one of her children living with her, and she had children my brother's age and mine, but when my grandmother needed wood, my father would get us, and we'd haul wood over there.

I'd be upset, because my aunt who was living there with my grandmother had sons, and those guys would be sitting up there, as big as I was, and they weren't trying to do anything to help themselves.

My mother said, "Y'all have got to understand, you're helping my mother, so don't worry about your rewards and what those guys are not doing. They've got to answer for the things that they do, and you've got to answer for the things that you do. If you help someone, the Lord is going to bless you."

As a man now who has children, I can look back on that, and I can see the Lord has blessed me in many ways.

When I was ten years old and in the fourth grade, I was over at my grandmother's house, playing in this tree with my cousin Jackie.

My aunt came out and said, "Y'all need to get out of that tree before one of y'all get hurt."

It's been said that God takes care of babies and fools. We had this piece of rubber—an elastic-type thing—we were using as a swing, and at the bottom of the tree was a barbed-wire fence.

Well, the thing would hold one of us, but when we put both of our weights on there and lowered it down, it broke and my blue jeans got caught on some barbed wire. I had a cousin, Gene Samuels, who was visiting, and he came out and tried to get me untangled from the barbed wire. My aunt also came over there. Before they got me untangled, blood started seeping through my blue jeans.

I said, "Hurry up!"

After they got me untangled, we pulled up my pants leg, and my leg was cut all the way to the bone.

My aunt said, "You're going to need stitches."

I started running, and my cousin picked me up and carried me to my parents' house. My mother took a cold towel and wrapped it around my leg.

They took me to Dr. Clinton, who had an office on White Street in town.

Dr. Clinton said, "I'm going to have to cut your leg off."

I said, "What?"

He said, "Yeah, this thing is cut to the bone," and it was. It was split all the way open, but he said, "I'm going to try to save it."

He put fifty stitches inside my leg and fifty stitches outside my leg. I had one hundred stitches in my leg. I have a long scar on my leg that I'll be carrying with me the rest of my life. As I grew bigger and have gotten older, the scar's gotten smaller, but it's still there.

When I went back to school, I couldn't go out to play. I could only look out the window and just watch them play. I had to wait until my leg healed.

I went to Buffalo, New York, with my grandmother Bessie Waiters and my cousin Howard Waiters, to spend the summer with my aunt. I had two aunts who lived in Buffalo.

When we got to Buffalo, N.Y., my grandmother was hesitant about letting me go anywhere. I couldn't do this and couldn't do that, but I had an older cousin up there named Wylie Mingo who was into some very interesting stuff, or so I thought. Back in the late '60s and early '70s, gangs were very prevalent. Wally was in a gang and into a lot of gang activities, so I wanted to be in a gang.

I would follow him wherever he went. When he went out there and got with them, he would lose me in the crowd.

When he'd come back I'd ask, "Man, why do you keep losing me? I want to see what's going on in these gangs."

He'd say, "No, I don't want you to be a part of it. The only reason I'm in it is because I don't want them to burn our house down with my mother in it."

I gave up on that right away.

I used to go down to the bakery at the corner at the end of the day, and they'd let me get all of the doughnuts they didn't sell for a quarter. Back then, you could get a lot for a quarter. You could buy a "Rock 'n Roll," which was two big ginger cake biscuits, a bag of potato chips, a Nehi soda—a grape or an orange—for a quarter and still have change left over. About twenty-two cents is what it would cost you. You could actually buy two cookies for a penny.

THE GREEN HORNET

Christmas was a special time of the year. We didn't get toys and things like that. We got basic necessities. One time, our cousins' and friends' parents bought them mini-bikes. Our parents couldn't afford to buy us a mini-bike. I remember I got one bicycle during my childhood. It was green, and I called it the "Green Hornet." I couldn't let anyone else ride my stuff and tear it up, because I wouldn't have had it anymore. I look back now, and at one time, my son had three bikes.

For Christmas, we'd get blue jeans and a pair of brogans. They call them Timberlands now, but they were called brogans back then. They were like construction boots. They had to last you all year.

I remember soon after my mother bought me shoes, my feet would start hurting. I didn't want to tell my mother my feet hurt, because she had just bought me the shoes. It got to the point of hurting so bad, my mother noticed and asked what was wrong.

I said, "My foot is hurting."

She said, "I just bought you those shoes," and she took me to town to Mr. Williams' shoe store. "I'm going to let you pick the shoes out this time, and you better not be complaining about your foot hurting."

We'd get the new shoes, and about three weeks later, my foot would start hurting again. My feet were outgrowing my body at the time.

She said, "You might not be the biggest son I have, but you have the biggest feet."

Still today, I have the biggest feet of any of my brothers. I wear size fourteen shoes. I'm probably one of the biggest sons she has, too.

That same year, I went to New York with my grandmother, and I had a growth spurt over the summer—my body was actually trying to catch up with my feet. When I returned, I had outgrown my brother Larry, and he's three years older than me. I towered over Larry, and my mom said, "I can't believe it."

JUST PAY US WHAT YOU FEEL

One time, when Larry and I were teenagers, a man was building a house and asked us to come over and help him clean up all the stuff that the contractors had left over—the bricks and rock and the mortar. He picked us up for several days and took us there. Even today, I see the house that he built. He passed away, but his wife still lives in the house. At the end of the week, Larry and I figured up what he owed us.

He asked us, "How much do I owe you?"

We thought about it and said, "Just pay us what you feel."

He told me something that I'll keep with me for the rest of my life.

He said, "First of all, let me tell you something you should always remember: Never tell anyone 'Just pay us whatever you feel,' because if you're doing a job—and doing a good job on it—you want to have a set price or an idea of what you're going to charge."

When he was young, he worked for this lady for a week, similar to what we had done.

At the end of the week, she asked, "How much do I owe you?" He said, "Just pay me what you feel."

She said, "Okay, well I feel like paying you a dollar," and that's what she paid him.

He really couldn't dispute it, because he asked her to pay him whatever she felt.

He said, "From now on, never say to anyone to pay you what he or she feels, because they might not feel like paying you anything."

He said to always give a set price or at least an idea of what you'll do it for.

Things always have a way of working out when you're obedient. Daddy always wanted us to get jobs, and I drove a school bus. I ended up going to all of the football games anyway, because I drove the bus. I also had a band run from the high school to the band room, and that was extra money. Even in high school, I found ways to haul someone and make extra money. Even though I wasn't playing, I was able to travel with the football team and go to all of the games so that kind of worked out okay.

THE DAYS OF MY LIFE

I was getting ready to go into high school, and I got my first job outside of school, working at Kentucky Fried Chicken on the bypass in Lancaster.

When I turned old enough to get my driver's license, I started driving a school bus, too. They showed us this film called *Death on the Highway*, which showed accidents and people getting hurt and maimed on buses. They asked us if we still wanted to drive.

About half the people walked out and said, "Forget that. I don't want that responsibility," but I was willing to take on the task, so I started driving school buses.

I had one group that lived in the Pardue Street Apartments, and a lot of them were on my first route to Southside Elementary School. They'd had three drivers quit on this route. There would be kids just showing out on the bus, and the drivers couldn't put up with it.

There I was, sixteen years old, on my first day driving the bus. The kids were showing out. They had let the windows down and were shouting—just having a good old time. It's like they were saying, "We've got new meat. I wonder how long he's going to last?"

I went into a curve and threw on the brakes, and some of them fell in the seats. I stopped, got up, and said, "See, if you're not sitting in your seats, that's how you could get hurt. So from here on out, you'd better be sitting down in a seat, and you better not be moving around. I better not hear anymore noise from you!" That broke those kids. I didn't have any problem with them whatsoever after that.

When the route around my area became available, I took it. The kids were begging me not to change, but I could make more money driving a route from my home than I could by driving an empty bus all the way into Lancaster, then picking up the kids and driving them home.

I learned a lot driving a bus. I had a lot of responsibility with those kids' lives; if you're doing it the right way, those kids will respect you. My senior year driving the bus, I was named the Outstanding Driver of the Year and won a scholarship. In fact, it was the first scholarship that they offered for driving a bus.

While I was in high school, my brother bought my mother a car—a '67 Ford Falcon. They sold the car to me, and I put a new engine in it, a paint job on it, and new tires. That was my little car. I was driving my little car to school. I had friends who were doing things like pulling up the emergency brake and spinning their tires.

I said, "Man, you're tearing up your car."

And they said, "Oh, my dad will buy me more tires."

I said, "You won't catch me burning up my tires, because my dad isn't going to buy mine. I have to pay for my own tires."

My car was sharp, with a souped-up engine, but I'd never speed in it or drive recklessly—nothing to tear up my vehicle.

My father had made a statement. He said he had six sons, and he wasn't going to buy any of them a car, nor was he going to buy any of his five daughters a car.

He said, "If you want a car, you're going to have to pay for it, and you're going to have to pay for your insurance. You're going to have to understand that you're responsible for the maintenance and upkeep of that vehicle."

If we tore it up, we didn't have anything. He stuck to his word. Our financial situation got better as children grew up and started their own families, but he still didn't buy any of us a car.

LESSONS LEARNED

In addition to working at KFC at sixteen years old, I had a little trash route. I'd go around and pick up trash for people in the Oak Ridge community and other areas. I'd provide them with a barrel, and they'd burn the trash, and I'd pick up the burnt trash. I'd go by every month to collect, and I'd give a part of the money to my father for the use of his truck, kind of like renting my father's truck.

With my trash business and my bus route, I was able to have a little bit of cash coming in. I was able to buy all of my school supplies, my class ring, my cap and gown, any books that I needed, and also my clothes while in school.

One guy on my route wouldn't pay me. He was nasty to me, saying, "Little boy, I am not going to pay you," so I went back and told my father.

He said, "I'll go talk to him."

When we went over there, my father said, "My son tells me you're on his trash route, and you're two months behind."

The guy said, "Yeah."

My father said, "Well, it's like this: You'll either pay him on Sunday, or you'll go to jail on Monday." The guy whipped out the money and paid me for the months he was behind.

My dad said, "By the way, you're not on his route anymore. He won't be picking up your trash anymore."

I wanted my dad to jump this guy because he had been talking junk to me. I didn't realize my dad was punishing him a lot more than if he had given him a licking, because now he was going to have to start taking his trash away himself or find somebody else to pick it up. He gave up the luxury he had and the low cost I was doing it for. He wasn't going to find anyone else to do it that cheap. He messed himself up.

I learned that you don't have to physically injure someone to get your point across. That's the kind of Christian person my father was.

The only time I can remember my father not going to church my whole life was the Sunday one of our hogs died. We had a hog that was pregnant with pigs, and she got out. She went into the back of our pasture. There was a guy who didn't like our family anyway, and he shot the hog. The hog made it back home. She had about sixteen piglets, but all of them died. Because their mother had been shot and went into labor too soon, she couldn't have a natural birth. That was devastating to our family because that hog lost sixteen pigs, and we lost her. That was a major financial blow to the family. This all happened on a Sunday morning.

The hog hadn't done anything to anybody. The hog wouldn't have hurt anyone, so it wasn't like this guy's life was in danger. There are evil people out there you've got to deal with.

This same guy said that Midnight had gotten into his corn. My brother Larry, and our cousin Kenneth Bell, and I went over there to check on him.

As we were walking into the cornfield, Larry said, "Wait a minute, let's step back," so we stepped back, and when we did, this guy just started shooting into the field. He was basically shooting at us, but we had stepped back into the wood line. If we had stayed in the field, we would have gotten shot.

We went back and told my father what had happened. He went over there and told the guy, "If you ever shoot at my sons again, you'll regret it."

This guy was an abuser. He used to abuse his wife a lot, and she had to come over to our house. Domestic violence was rampant in that home. My mother tried to tell her she didn't need to put up with that and needed to get out of there. Later on, when I went into the service, my father told me he shot her with a shotgun and then killed himself. She never did get out of there.

My father used to cut our hair all the time. Since I felt I was growing up, I wanted a change. I let my cousin braid my hair. She put it into little "Buckwheat" braids, and those things hurt because she had them real tight.

My father said, "What are you trying to do?"

I said, "I might want to try to grow an Afro."

He said, "No. You're not going to grow one." My dad used to give us military haircuts.

We asked Mom if she'd try to talk Dad into letting me grow an Afro.

He said, "No, you're not going to do it. Y'all will be running around here with your hair all nappy and everything."

I said, "No dad, it won't happen."

He said, "Well, the first time I see it nappy, it's coming off."

During my junior year, my sister Denise would braid my hair every night, and every day I'd take my braids loose and comb my hair out. One day, I was running late and didn't get a chance to take the braids out. I was taking sociology, and Mr. David Jenkins was my teacher.

No boy had ever worn braids in the school. I was in class, and Mr. Jenkins said, "Did you forget something?"

I said, "No."

"Well, what about those braids in your hair?"

"What about them?"

"You need to take those braids out of your hair."

"Why?"

"Because you need to take them out." There was no school policy about it. I wasn't trying to be rebellious about it.

He said, "You've got five minutes to take those braids out of your hair, or I'm going to write you up as having an unexcused absence from my class."

I said, "I don't have a pick."

"Well, you've got ten minutes to find a pick and get those braids out of your hair."

The other students said, "No, Kevan, don't do it. He can't make you do it."

I said, "Sir, my mother has seen these braids. They're neat, and I don't think there's anything wrong with it."

He said, "Well, you need to go take them out. So you need to leave my class and go take those braids out."

I walked down the hall. I didn't want to be rebellious, but I was thinking about it. I hadn't done anything wrong. There was nothing wrong with my braids. I decided not to take them out, so I just didn't go back to that class. Rumors started going around the school. Everyone was watching to see how long it would be before they made me take out the braids. I went to my next class and didn't have a problem there. I went to lunch, and they called the superintendent to the school. They wanted him to talk to me.

In the meantime, I checked school policy, and there was no policy about it. I wasn't violating any school rules, and they couldn't just make the rules up. They couldn't enforce something that wasn't even there.

My next class after lunch was algebra. I was in the cafeteria, going through the line. I sat down at a table, and the superintendent sat down beside me.

He said, "I didn't know if you were a girl or a boy."

I said, "Excuse me, sir?"

He said, "I didn't know if you were a girl or a boy."

I said, "Well, I'm a boy."

He said, "Well, I didn't know it with those braids in your hair."

I said, "Well, I'm a boy."

He said, "You've got until the end of lunch period to have those braids out of your hair," and I didn't say anything. "Do you hear me?"

I said, "Yes sir. I hear you."

He said, "You've got until the end of lunch to have those braids out of your hair."

So I went to algebra. I was sitting there, and he busted into the class. Well, the braids were still in. I ended up wearing the braids the rest of the day, and it actually started a trend where all of the boys who had long hair started wearing their hair braided.

Now, when I look back at it, I understand why they didn't want me to do that. There were people coming in with bad braids, and they were making it look bad. Some guys had jobs at the Bleachery and the mill, and they had gotten cotton in their hair and their braids while they were at work. While mine was neat and clean, they were coming in there nappy, so I understand why they didn't want me to open that can of worms.

I was told that when my brother Ernest went to college, he didn't know how to iron or cook because he had a couple of sisters behind him, and they did all of the cooking and the ironing.

When he came back and told my mother that his roommate Cleo knew how to cook and iron, she said, "That's it. None of my boys will ever leave home again without knowing how to cook or iron."

Once, my brother Larry and I were ironing our clothes and accidentally spilled some bleach on our blue jeans. It gave them a faded look. Later on, we saw stores were selling them like that. We said, "Man, we need to try to get some royalties on that."

I graduated from Lancaster High School in 1975, and I had scholarships to go to college. I wanted to be an electrical engineer. I had taken mechanical drafting, Spanish, Algebra, Latin, Psychology, and Sociology, but I wanted to pursue a career in electrical engineering. That's where my focus was upon graduating from high school.

After I graduated, I started working at the Springs River Lawn plant in Fort Lawn, South Carolina, another Springs Industries company.

When I first went looking for a job, some of my friends and I went together to apply. When I was leaving, one of the guys doing the interview called me and said, "Let me give you a couple of job tips."

I said, "What's that?"

He said, "First of all, when you go looking for a job, don't go looking with a group. If the guy only has one job, he's not sure which one of you is the best worker, so he's not going to hire anyone out of the group. If you go looking by yourself, you may be able to find a job, because if he only has one, you may be able to get it."

I took that as a hint and came back the next day, and I got a job as a locator at the plant. I worked through the summer, and when the fall came, I enrolled in electrical engineering at York Technical College. I was working full-time at Springs River Lawn plant and going to school full-time at York Technical College.

My days were full. Between school and work, I didn't have time for anybody. A lot of my friends would come by and say, "Man, why are you wasting your time going to school? High school was all I needed."

I said, "I want to better my life and better myself.".

At the plant, I drove something called a Raymond—it is like a backward forklift—and I had to put up all these different boxes.

They made a lot of drapes, bedspreads, and things like that, and I'd put them in the warehouse. A classmate of mine was working there too.

He came flying out of the warehouse. I blew my horn to tell him I was up in the air locating a box and couldn't get out of his way, because he was coming too fast. He flew through there, ran into my buggy, and tore the top of the forklift off. It tossed me around in the buggy like a rag doll. I was hurt, but I didn't want anyone to know it because I didn't want my classmate to get fired. That classmate didn't turn out too well, so maybe I should have pursued and collected on that.

I had another coworker who was in school with me also. He came home from work and caught his girl with another guy. He didn't think he could live without her, so he drank some antifreeze and coffee. His mother came home, found him passed out, and took him to the hospital. They pumped the poison out and saved him. He got kicked out of school because he missed too many days, and they were thinking of firing him at work because he was suicidal.

He started seeing a psychiatrist and talked to me about it.

I asked, "Why did you do that?"

He said, "I didn't want to live anymore."

"Why do you want to do something like that? That's crazy. You could have gone and bought yourself some Jack Daniels, drank that, and passed out, not gone out there and had antifreeze." If he hadn't mixed that coffee with it, he probably wouldn't be here today.

I got a lot of overtime at the plant. I'd work weekends when other people would want to take off. I had a goal in mind, and I was working hard toward it.

My brother Larry, who was living in Washington, DC, at the time, came down. He told me they had a plan in the military where we could go in under the buddy plan. He wanted us to join the Air Force.

Ernest, D. Frank, and Joe had all gone into the army, and they all were drafted. I told Larry I wasn't too interested in going into the military. He said, "Let's go take the test and go into the Air Force under the buddy plan and let the Air Force pay for your college."

We decided to go to Rock Hill, in South Carolina, to take the test. On the way, we passed a Marine Corps recruitment office and talked with them. We went back home, and Larry left and went back to Washington, DC. A few days later, the Marine recruiter called me and asked, "Why do you want to go into the Air Force?"

I didn't really know much about the service other than my brothers going into the army. I didn't know anything about the Marine Corps.

I said, "The Air Force has good bases." All I knew is what Larry had told me.

He asked, "So what do you want to do in life?"

I said, "There are three things I want to accomplish in life: I want to travel and see the world, I want to finish my education, and I'd like to get paid while I'm doing it."

He said, "You can do all of that in the Marines. You can travel and see the world. You can complete your education, and you can get paid while you're doing it."

He said the Marines would promote me on my ability, and I'd have a chance to excel at a faster rate than any of the other branches. He convinced me, so I went in and signed up for the Marines.

My parents did not have to sign for me. I had turned eighteen that summer, but the recruiter wanted my parents to be involved in what was going on. We had just been through a lot of drama in Vietnam, looking at the mail everyday and hoping our guys would come back. One of my cousins stepped on a mine, and that made my mother even more worried.

At one point, when Ernest and D. Frank were in Vietnam, they sent Joe to Panama for jungle training to go to Vietnam.

When my parents wrote my brothers and told them he was in Panama training, they said, "Look, they're training him to come to Vietnam."

My parents hopped in the car and drove to the Pentagon. They told them, "You got two of our sons already over there. And now you want to send a third one to Vietnam? No."

That's when they changed his orders from Vietnam and sent him to South Korea instead, so he was in Korea, and they were in Vietnam. That was a lot for my parents to handle at one time. I wasn't sure if they were going to be antimilitary or not, but they were supportive.

Break Them and Build Them

On March 16, 1976, I joined the Marines, and I decided to take some time off and go on a vacation. I was going to spend about two weeks on vacation and then go to boot camp. I was scheduled to leave to go to boot camp on March 28, 1976.

I left and went to Washington, DC, to go on vacation. My cousin and I bought bus tickets and took the bus to Washington. We had been in Washington for a couple of days. I was over at my cousin's house visiting them when we got a phone call; my cousin was freaking out and crying.

I said, "What's going on? What's wrong?"

My uncle had passed. He had a heart attack. Uncle R.B. was the closest man to me after my father, so that was pretty tough. We came home and had his funeral. The day after his funeral, I went to boot camp, but I was in shock from my uncle's funeral.

On the trip there, we stopped in Columbia, where they picked us up and carried us through the medicals. They drew our blood. The guy ahead of me was a big, 250-pound man, and he obviously couldn't handle the sight of blood. He just fell on the floor.

Once we went through that, they waited until later and put us on a Greyhound bus. We stopped somewhere in Columbia.

One of the guys on the bus had been in the army before, and was going to the Marines. He ran over to a liquor store and bought some gin. None of the rest of us were old enough to buy alcohol. On the way to Parris Island, he gave us a little sip.

When we got there, they didn't take us right onto the island. They waited until about one or two in the morning. When the bus stopped, a drill instructor got on and yelled at us to get off the bus and go stand on these yellow footprints painted on the sidewalk.

We got off the bus and stood on the yellow footprints. They took us into this building and made us come to attention on our knees. The drill instructor walked on a table. He asked us if we took any drugs or anything illegal in the past twenty-four hours.

We replied, "No sir!"

"We're going to do a urine analysis on you, and if you've got any drugs in you, you'll be going home."

They told us to lie down for a little bit. We went to lie down, and this guy jumped up and had an epileptic fit. He was shaking and everything. Someone got a spoon and put in his mouth. We never saw him again.

The next day we had the same clothes on, and they were getting pretty rough. We finally picked out our uniforms, and they took us to get our hair cut. They asked what style of haircut we wanted, but they were going to cut our hair off anyway—there wasn't going to be any style to it.

I think drill instructors aren't human, because when you wake up, they are already awake, and when you go to sleep, they are still awake.

The second night, in the same platoon I was in, a guy freaked out and started running in the middle of the night. The drill instructor grabbed the guy, and they started fighting, and this other guy—a big guy—started helping the recruit fight the drill instructor because it looked like the drill instructor was going to hurt this kid. Another drill instructor came up, and they got everything straightened out and took the recruit out of there.

The next day, they put numbers in a hat. They said they were doing a new survey. We didn't know it at the time, but they were breaking us up. Initially, I was in platoon 3329. When I pulled a number, I got thirty-one. The next day, I was sent to thirty-one, and my new drill instructor was named Sgt. Carter.

Carter was good at drilling, but he was a tough guy. After about two weeks, we'd been yelling so much we were hoarse. Carter told us to get online. When he gave us an order, we would yell, "Sir, yes, sir!"

He told us to get on line. We were on line already.

He looked over at a recruit across from me, Private Wright. We were in alphabetical order, so he was right across from me.

He said, "Oh, Private Wright isn't yelling. I can't see his jugular veins moving." He went over there and got in his face.

He said, "Private Wright, get on line!"

Wright said, "Sir, yes, sir!"

He said, "Louder!"

"Sir, yes, sir!"

"Louder!"

"Sir, yes, sir!"

"I don't see your jugular vein moving. Say it again."

He did this over and over, and I saw Wright's fist ball up.

I was moving my lips, mouthing, *No! No! Don't do it!*

I could see that Wright was losing his cool.

Next thing I knew, Wright hit him right in the nose. It knocked his glasses off, and his nose started bleeding. The drill instructor grabbed him and shoved him up against the locker, then let him go, saying, "No, you're not worth it."

They walked out.

They put us in a circle and told us if we hit a drill instructor we could go to jail.

They next day some of the biggest MPs I've ever seen in my life came in there. They were six-foot-four—all of them.

They said, "We're looking for Private Wright."

They grabbed his sea bag, tied it to him, and dragged him out of there. We never saw Wright again after that.

My Marine Corps recruit training was broken down into three phases. The first phase was conditioning and academics. They broke us down and then built us back up. The second phase was the rifle range and maintenance, and the third phase was jungle warfare training, academics and trying on our uniforms. We did a lot of big inspections, and we ran a lot.

The first phase seemed the hardest, but the third phase was actually the most difficult. By then, we were acclimated to the island and had built up our physical attributes. At that point, we felt we could do anything.

We went out to take our Initial Strength Test—a physical fitness test. They had little plastic tags they put on our shirts. It had "sit-ups," "pull-ups" and "run" written on it. They wrote our scores with a grease pencil on that little tag. Then, we went to the instructor, and he'd write it down on a clipboard. Then, Sergeant Carter went over to the pull-up bars to demonstrate how to do a pull-up properly.

He said, "When I tell you to, I want you to mount the bar and come to a dead hang. I'm going to tell you to begin, and you'll pull your body weight over the bar. You come back down with your elbows locked, and you'll come back up and do as many as you can. Once you've done as many as you can, you come back to a dead hang, and I'll tell you to dismount the bar."

I was probably the sixth or seventh person in line, and everybody who got up there couldn't do more than nine pull-ups. Some did four, some did five, but the most anyone did was nine.

When I got to the bar, Carter said, "Mount the bar."

I mounted the bar and came to a dead hang, and I pumped about twenty pull-ups. I was so excited, I jumped off the bar.

He said, "Didn't I tell you to come to a dead hang?"

I looked at him like a deer caught in headlights. I said, "Sir, yes, sir."

He said, "When I tell you to come to a dead hang, that's what I mean," and he wrote "3" on my card.

I couldn't believe it.

We went to do sit-ups. If we did eighty sit-ups in less than two minutes, we got one hundred points. For every pull-up we did, we got five points. Instead of having one hundred points on the pull-ups, I only got fifteen points, which was the minimum. We had to do at least three.

On the sit-ups, they blew a whistle and started a stopwatch. They gave us two minutes.

I pumped out sixty-something sit-ups. When I got done, Carter came over and wrote "25" on my chest.

I thought, *Oh my goodness—this guy is going to make me fail this test.*

Then, we had to run a mile and a half.

I knew I had to do really well on the run, or it wouldn't work out like I expected.

I ran and beat everyone else. I ran up to the senior drill instructor and had him write my time before Carter could get to it. My time was good, and it was the only thing that saved me.

So, when we got back to the barracks, I was put on remedial physical training because I couldn't do but three pull-ups. I couldn't tell the senior drill instructor that Carter had only given me three. I didn't understand what he had done, and I hated him.

While everybody else was writing letters home, I had to do pull-ups. I did pull-ups and pull-ups and more pull-ups. They had this exercise equipment called a bull worker, and I was working with that, averaging 200 pull-ups a night. I got so good I started teaching the other guys who were weak on pull-ups how to do pull-ups.

When we did our next test, I aced it and won a phone call home.

One day, they had a hygienic inspection. All we had on were shower shoes and a towel. They made us drop the towels, and they looked to see if we had any bruises on our hips or blisters on our heels from our boots that we weren't saying anything about.

A guy named London was next to me. Carter had punched him in the stomach, and he had yellow bruises.

When the commander asked where he got the marks from, he answered, "Sgt. Carter, sir," and that was it.

They got Carter from home and put him up for court martial. They had tried to get Carter before, and that was like the final straw.

When I won the fitness test the next time, they gave me an award for most improvement and let me call home. They asked me if I had been shamming the first time or if I had improved that much. I thought about all those pull-ups I had done and then said, "I improved."

PRAY FOR RAIN

I got through first phase. We had to do a six- or seven-mile march out to the rifle range. We walked and sang with our helmets, packs, and rifles. It was a really fast walk. We got out of that and had a field meet. We had five events, and they had me in four of them—a four-mile run and things like that. It was a lot of fun; it was like letting us relax a little bit, but the next day, my leg started swelling really badly.

The whole time I had been there—I got on the island in March, and now it was May—it hadn't rained. It was beautiful weather—eighty-five or ninety degrees, no clouds anywhere. We were out there doing something called "snapping in." They had barrels painted white with black dots. They showed us all of the positions we would have to shoot in. We were out there doing sitting, kneeling, prone position and the offhand. My leg was hurting me then, but I was trying to learn how to get in those positions.

We fired into the black dots by looking into our back sights. We had to line it up with the dot in the front sight. We shot either M16s or A1 rifles.

It looked kind of stupid at first, because we were only a few feet from the barrel, but when you're firing at 500 yards away, the target looks like that little black dot, so it makes sense.

The third day into the training, they did the hygienic inspection again, and my right leg was swollen. The commander looked at it and said, "You need to go to sick bay in the morning and get your leg checked out."

The next day, I went to the clinic, which was maybe about five miles from where we were. They x-rayed my leg, and I had a stress fracture. The doctor said it was from all of the walking and running I had done at one time. I had been giving it one hundred percent and had cracked a bone in my right leg.

He said, "I'm going to have to put you on three days' light duty."

I was excited because I thought I wouldn't have to do any push-ups or jumping jacks, side-straddle hops or sit-ups like the rest of them, and I was going to get three days off.

Everyone in training has what is called a PMI—primary marksmanship instructor—who works with them and teaches them to shoot. The drill instructors step back and let the PMIs handle it.

Each PMI has about ten guys he works with, and he works with them the whole time. I handed the PMI the chit for three days' light duty.

When I handed it to him, he looked at it and said, "Kevan, I'm sorry."

I said," What's wrong?"

He said, "You can't snap in on light duty."

Our new drill instructor, Staff Sgt. Drake, was standing off in the back and he said, "I heard that. Waiters, go pack your trash."

I was walking back to the barracks, my head down. This was the lowest point in my life. I couldn't believe this was happening. I thought I was going to have to go to what we called MRP—medical rehabilitation platoon—and I just didn't think I could handle it. I thought I was going to lose all my friends. I didn't know how long it was going to take for my leg to heal. I didn't think that mentally, I'd be able to handle it once I got there. I went from being happy and being excited to the lowest point in my life.

Anyway, every time we left the barracks, we left one person behind for fire watch. He saw me and asked what I was doing there.

I told him Drake told me to pack my trash.

He said, "What are you going to do?"

I said, "I don't know, man. I'm going to wait until the senior drill instructor comes."

Walking back, the weather was about ninety degrees. It was beautiful.

Some of the guys walked by and asked, "Waiters, what are you going to do?"

I said, "I don't know. I'm going to talk to the senior drill instructor." The senior drill instructor was like a father figure. "I'm going to wait and talk to him. I don't know what I'm going to do."

A second guy came by and asked me the same thing and I gave him the same answer.

The third guy walked by and asked me the same question, but this time, the Spirit came to me and said, *Pray for rain.*

I kind of wondered what this had to do with anything, and I heard it again. *Pray for rain.*

When the third guy left, the fourth guy came up and said, "Waiters, what are you going to do?"

I said, "Pray for rain."

He said, "Pray for *rain?* What's rain got to do with this?"

"You asked me what I'm going to do, and that's what I'm going to do. The Spirit told me to pray for rain."

He said, "Well, you've got to have clouds before it can rain. Did you see any out there?"

"No."

"Ain't nothing but stars up there. Man, it hasn't rained the whole time we've been on the island. Pray for rain?"

I said, "Well, you asked me what I'm going to do, and that's what I'm going to do."

By this time, they were passing it around to each other saying, "Waiters is going to pray for rain." They were all looking at me like I was crazy.

They said, "Praying for rain? What's rain got to do with this?"

We laid down about ten o'clock and went to sleep.

About two o'clock in the morning, everybody woke up to a sound hitting the top of the building. It was rain!

I sat up, and rain was just pouring down on the building. Everyone sat up in the rack and looked at me, and I looked at them. I was at the very end because I was a squad leader. No one said anything. They all just lay back down and said, "Oh my God! This guy is powerful!"

The atmosphere in the room was eerie. The guys were thinking, *We're scared of him.*

That morning when Drake woke up for us to go to breakfast, he opened the door, and the rain came pouring in. He said, "Where did this rain come from? It wasn't in the forecast. How did this rain get here?"

He said, "Well, I'm not getting wet. Y'all just run over there and eat breakfast, and don't get wet. Try not to fall. Just eat breakfast and come back."

We ran over, ate breakfast, and came back.

He told us we were going to have to snap in the barracks. He forgot about me, and I didn't say anything to him. I kept my mouth shut.

It rained for three days.

Making of a Man

Don't tell God how big your problem is;
tell your problem how big your God is!

After that, I continued and qualified. It was tough getting into those positions because my leg was hurting, but I got in them anyway, and I made it through.

In first and second phase, the platoon had a yellow flag with red letters, but if eighty-five percent of the platoon scored well, they got a red flag with yellow lettering. We scored well, so we got the red flag with yellow lettering, and we got a choice between mess and maintenance. We chose maintenance. All I did was hang around the general's building for a week. I dumped his ashtrays and things like that. It was like a week of vacation.

After that, we went to the next phase. We started running four miles, then five. We were running every day, and PT was very hard. My leg started swelling up again, and they said, "You need to go back to sick bay and have them to check your leg out."

When I went back over there, it had cracked some more. The doctor told me that if I kept running, I would break it, and that could cripple me. He suggested I go on to the third-phase stress fracture program. He told me I couldn't do anymore PT, just class and the academic stuff, but no more physical stuff. He told me they'd still let me graduate, but I didn't have to do anymore of the physical stuff. I didn't think they would have a problem with signing it.

There was already a guy in our platoon on that program, and they called him "Crip." They treated him like crap, like dirt. It would be like, "Well, come on Crip." He was marching and limping. I couldn't see myself being treated like that. I didn't want to be treated like that. I was trying to make a decision on my way back about whether or not I should turn in the form. I didn't turn it in.

I told my bunkie about it, and he said, "You're disobeying a lawful order because a commander in the navy gave you that slip, and you're not turning it in."

I said, "Well, I'm just going to have to take the chance."

The doctor already told me that he was going to call and check on me to see how I was doing.

Every time they called my name, I was on pins and needles, afraid they had caught me and I was going to be in trouble. Even when they called my name for mail call, I'd be worried and was shaking.

I kept it to myself. My bunkmate was the only other one who knew. I'd look to see who was the last fire watch every shift, and I'd have him wake me up forty-five minutes before everybody else every day. I'd wrap my leg up because you only have between a minute and two minutes to get dressed, and I couldn't wrap my leg and get dressed that fast.

It was getting worse, but I was just trying to suck it up and get through with it.

We had only one week left in running, and we had gotten up to running five miles a day by then.

After that, we were going to have two weeks of trying on uniforms, getting fitted and things like that. It was winding down and getting pretty close to graduation.

I thought if I could just make it through this week with the training, I'd be okay. We were going to have at least four more days of running, and then we were going to be off that Friday.

On Monday, we went out and ran the five miles. My leg was killing me the whole time. When we got back, we were standing there, and our canteens were staged on the ground. They tell you when you can get a drink of water. By this time, it was June, and it was hot. We were standing beside the canteens, and the nerves in my leg suddenly went crazy. My leg was shaking, and it suddenly just jumped up in the air, maybe a foot off of the ground, and it was just shaking.

Drake looked at me and yelled, "Waiters, put your foot down!"

I put my foot down, and it popped back up because the nerves were just going haywire. It was scaring me because it had never gotten that bad.

He ran down to me and said, "What's wrong with you?"

I had to tell him. I didn't have any other choice at this point, because my leg was just going crazy.

I said, "Sir, this recruit has a stress fracture, sir."

He didn't say anything; he just walked away.

The next day, I woke up early again. I was wrapping it and told my bunkie I didn't know if I was going to make it.

I said, "My leg has never been this bad before. I don't know if it can make it."

PT gear is shorts, a shirt, and tennis shoes. We made left face and right face, and then we were ready to march out of there.

Drake said, "Double time!" and we would all run out.

We got ready. We made a left face, a right face, and he said, "Double time!" but right before he said that, he said, "Waiters, fall out. You're barracks watch," and I stayed back.

I said, "Thank you, God!"

That was one day I needed off. I thought if I could just get to Friday, we wouldn't have to do anymore of that running. We'd only have our final two weeks with that little bit of PT, and three miles was nothing, but five miles was murder on it.

They went out for PT that day and came back. The next day, Wednesday, our third day of PT, we were getting ready to go out. I knew he couldn't let me be on barracks watch again that day because, if he did, everyone would know he was showing favoritism toward me. I thought it wasn't going to happen.

We did the facial movements, and he said, "Double time!" We went out and staged our canteens on the ground.

There were four platoons in a series and about sixty recruits in each platoon, so we had about 240 recruits.

While we were in formation and getting ready to take off and run, Drake yelled, "Waiters, be gear watch!"

No one had ever watched the gear the whole time I'd been there. I thought, *Thank you, God!* I realized he was helping me, but he was doing it in a nonchalant way where no one would know he was helping me.

I stayed out there, and I was the gear watch. They ran and came back, and I was wondering what he was going to do for Thursday. It was going to be my third day—there goes that three again—and I thought, "If I can just get through Thursday."

I was wondering how he could get me out of the running again. Those two days were a blessing.

The next morning, we were getting dressed, and he came over to me and told me not to get dressed out.

"I need for you to take a message down to the general's building," he said. He sent me as a messenger boy to the general's building. He saved me. I thank God now when I look back on how he used each avenue to not let on to the platoon about giving me that break.

With those three days, I was able to complete the training. My leg had really had it; it wasn't going to take too much more. If I'd had to run those three days, those miles would have done me in.

I ended up graduating with the stress fracture. When I was home on leave, I didn't do any kind of running. I kept my leg elevated and kept ice on it. I just basically let it heal.

WEST COAST, EAST COAST

When I got to California, my first duty station, they said they needed for me to come in and let them x-ray my leg to see how it was doing. So they x-rayed my leg and it had healed almost perfectly.

They said, "They did a good job of helping heal your leg at Parris Island." I wasn't going to tell them the truth about what really happened.

I spent June through September in California. I had orders for northern California, but I was in love with a girl, Miss Watts, back in South Carolina who was still in high school, so I decided to try to get closer to the East Coast.

I had a friend who had orders to Charleston, so I switched orders with him and moved back. I was stationed at the Polaris Nuclear Facility in Goose Creek, South Carolina. I thought the Lord had punished me by sending me there, because we were in the middle of nowhere.

In the meantime, the girl I was in love with, Miss Watts, didn't know what my plans were. I wanted to eventually get back into school and get married. I guess I didn't tell her that, and this guy started hanging around, telling her he'd be there. I came home one weekend, and she told me she didn't want to see me anymore. I was devastated.

I went back and started going to the weight room. I ran five miles a day for about six months. I gained twenty-five pounds of muscle; I was up to about 195 pounds.

I hadn't called home in six months, and my mother called the Red Cross. The Colonel called me into his office. He asked me how long had it been since I talked with my mother. I told him it had been about six months.

He said, "You're correct. Call your mother right now."

He handed me the phone, and I called my mother. When I hung up with her, he said, "Boy, if you ever pull that stunt again, not letting your mother know where you are or how you are doing, you're going to have to answer to me."

I went home and stopped at a service station on Springdale Road. While I was inside, my father pulled up to pump his gas. I told the cashier I'd pay for his gas, too. He was walking into the store as I was walking out.

I said, "How are you doing, sir?"

He said, "How are you doing, young man?" He didn't even recognize me.

He went in to pay for his gas, and the cashier told him I had already paid for it. He came back out, saw my car, and recognized it.

I said, "You're going to walk right past your son and not even recognize him?"

He said, "Boy, I can't believe how big you've gotten."

"Wait until I tell Mom you didn't even know your own son."

I came home and sat down in my living room. My father told me to come into the bedroom so he could talk to me for a minute. My father was about five-foot- eight, and he weighed probably about 185 pounds. I'm six-foot-one and 195. I came in there and said, "Yes, sir?"

My father really shocked me. He reached back and knocked the daylights out of me, in my chest. He knocked the wind out of me. I fell over and got up. I couldn't believe what just happened. He said, "Let me explain something to you. I don't care how big you get; I'm still your father." We both laughed it off.

I was stationed in Charleston from August 1976 to May 1979. In 1977, I was in the park, and I met this young lady. We kind of hit it off really well. Everything was going really well. We started seeing each other on a regular basis. Her name was Suzanne, and we dated for a couple of months, and I fell in love with her.

Then, her friends told me that Suzanne was married. I questioned her. I said, "Suzanne, are you married?"

"No," she said, "My friends just told you that because they want to get with you."

I was so much in love, I really didn't think a whole lot about it.

About five months into the relationship, she said, "I need to tell you something."

I said, "Okay, let me brace myself. What do you need to tell me?"

She said, "Well, I am pregnant."

Oh, man. I was so excited about it, you know. I cared for her, and I felt like she cared for me, so everything was going well.

A month later she said, "I need to tell you something else."

I thought, *what could be more exciting than telling me she was pregnant?*

Then, she told me she was married, and her husband was on his way home. Her husband had been on a submarine for six months. Finally, it dawned on me that she never needed money or anything.

She always had funds, but she wasn't working. That was kind of strange, but with the crazy hours I was working at the Polaris Nuclear Facility, I didn't pay much attention to it. I should have. I guess I was more in love than really paying attention to the signs that she was married.

I was devastated. I asked, "What are you going to tell your husband?"

She said, "Well, I am going to have this baby."

"Why didn't you tell me you were married?"

"Would you have continued to see me?"

"No."

"That's why I didn't tell you. But I am going to have your baby. I am going to have your baby. I don't love him, and I want to be with you."

I said, "You're going to do me like you did him?"

I had to go out on six-month tour, too, so I was pretty done with it. I pretty much just left her alone. A year passed by. One of my friends was in downtown Charleston, and he ran into Suzanne, and she was pushing this baby.

He looked at the baby and said, "That baby looks just like Waiters."

She asked, "Is Waiters still around?"

He said, "Yeah."

"Tell him I need to see him."

He came back and said, "Man, you are not going to believe this. Guess who I saw in downtown Charleston pushing a baby carriage?"

I said, "Man, that sounds like one of those Marine Corps hymns: *She pushed the baby carriage in the month of May/She pushed it for that young Marine so far, far away.* Man, you have got to be kidding me."

He said, "No, she said she wanted to see you."

I went down there and saw her, and she was with her parents. She had a little girl, Marie, and she was beautiful. She looked just like me.

She told her parents, "I don't want anything from him, or nothing like that, but I just want to let him know. Every man should know if he's got a child. This is his child." Then, to me, she said, "I am telling you in front of my parents that this is your daughter."

I asked her, "Well, then, you know, am I going to be able to see her? You know, later on."

She said, "Well, when she gets to be six years old I will let you see her."

Six years passed by, and I had gotten married. I hadn't started a family yet, but I was getting ready. I called her up to ask about seeing her. I talked with her, and she told me that she'd had two more children.

I said, "Well, what has your husband said?"

She said, "Well, he noticed the difference in the children's complexion."

My daughter was a little different than the other two children, and I am not sure what she really told him.

At that point, I was just starting my relationship with my wife, and it wasn't really a good time. I backed off, and even today, I haven't seen or talked to her since then.

I have had her on my heart and thought about her and really contemplated doing some research to find out where she is. I don't really know what kind of controversy it may cause, but a lot of my friends are saying, "Contact her. You need to contact her."

Charleston was an experience for me. I met a lot of good people in Charleston, but it was not the true Marine Corps I had expected. My Colonel said I needed to experience the fleet and get out and see parts of the world I had never seen before. A lot of people weren't reenlisting. They had about a three percent reenlistment rate. When I was there, I played all-star football, baseball, basketball. I also boxed. I was able to fulfill my dream of playing the sports I didn't get to play in high school.

We had pretty good teams, too. Some of them went undefeated until we met teams from other branches in the regional finals. We could never beat the Air Force in basketball. We could never beat the navy in football, because they had so many more people to choose from.

We were playing this Myrtle Beach team in basketball, the Myrtle Beach Air Force, and they had a guy on there who must have been Michael Jordan's cousin—the guy was real good. He was running rings around us. Alone, he was beating us.

When we played the navy, we were playing ships with five or six thousand people to choose from—that's a lot of people. Some of the smaller players on their team were my size, and everybody else was bigger.

As far as our region, though, we were undefeated. I enjoyed the time I spent there.

The Quiet Before the Storm

Headhunters and Cannibals

For my next duty station, I went to Okinawa, Japan. It's an island about eighty miles long. It has an Air Force base and several Marine Corps camps on it. One of the camps I went to was Camp Swab, at the farthest point of the island. After Camp Swab, there's nothing left up there except places you're prohibited from visiting. There are headhunters—cannibals—in some of those areas, and we couldn't go there. Camp Swab was on the beach area of the island. It was beautiful, but it was in the middle of nowhere, away from everything and the main attractions.

After getting there, they told me not to even unpack my sea bag because we were getting ready to go to the Philippines for ninety days on a float. We left there, and when we got to the Philippines, we were scheduled to do a lot of jungle training. Then, the monsoon season kicked in. It was raining every day.

We initially went out into the field, but it started raining so badly that we could hardly do any training. We stayed soaking wet all day, every day, so they decided to pull us in. We had been out in the rain for about three days. The water ruined our sea rations.

We had what they called a rubber lady, a rubber mattress we slept on since we were sleeping on the ground. Our rubber ladies were floating, so they decided it was too dangerous to stay out there. They started bringing helicopters in and airlifting all of the companies out of there, but our commanding officer decided that since we had walked over there, we could walk back. It was about a twenty-five-mile march, and we had to go over this thing called the "Seven Steps of Heaven," these different tiers we had to cross to get up this mountain. Everyone else was getting airlifted, and we were going back the way we came. It was so wet and muddy that going back across the Seven Steps of Heaven, we slid down. We couldn't even stay on our feet to walk it. When we got to the bottom, some trucks picked us up and took us back to the base.

They decided they'd just hold a lot of classes, and they set up a guard system so that when the rain stopped, they could go back to training again.

With my experience being in the Marine barracks, they decided to make me the Sergeant of the Guard. I set the schedule and made all of the arrangements. I was told to pick some guys I wanted to work with, and however I set it up was up to me. I set up a two-day system. I picked another Sergeant. I told him I'd work two days, and he'd work two days, so we would work two days and be off two. We had a rotation. I had four shifts with the troops, and it worked out pretty well.

I was so good at being the Sergeant of the Guard, that whoever the officer of the day was got a little extra help. The officer of the day would have to come back to the base to make sure the security was okay. The officers would actually wager to try to get officer of the day whenever I was on duty. I had my system down so well they would just come in and go to sleep, and I'd take care of everything. When they would wake up, their logbook would be done. It was really like a break for them.

After the three months were finished there, we came back to Okinawa to get ready to go to cold-weather training in Korea. This was during the Iran Crisis in 1979. They were going to initially send us into Iran to get those hostages they had taken. This was going to be my first opportunity to be involved in a wartime situation, but they decided to wait. At the time, Jimmy Carter was the president—this was late September 1979.

The United States started having a major conflict with Korea. Koreans didn't want any Americans on their streets, and they locked the bases down. That's where they had planned to train us, but then they said we weren't going to go into Korea because it was too dangerous. They sent us to Mount Fuji, Japan. We got our cold-weather training there.

About this time, Hurricane David hit the island. We had already gotten on a ship, but they pulled us off and put us back in the barracks. We stayed in the barracks for about three days. They shut everything down because of the hurricane. We were eating sea rations.

They put us back on the ship after about three days. They said that if the hurricane hit while we were at sea, we could outrun it. That didn't happen.

Each aircraft carrier came with escorts. They each had a submarine and 2 boats called LSTs (Land Sea Transport Vehicles). They'd protect the outer barrier of the carrier, which had tanks, Harriers and helicopters. There were about five thousand people on this carrier. It was like a big mall on the water.

On the ship, we ate in color codes—red, green, yellow, and blue. My color was blue. When we got through with breakfast, they were getting ready to serve the red group lunch. By the time we ate lunch, they were about ready to serve red dinner.

A lot of times on the ship, most of what we did was eat. Because the ship was so big and had so many people, it took all day to feed everybody.

Periodically, we would do different operations off of the ship. As we were traveling to Mount Fuji, the hurricane caught up with us. It was beating us up left and right out there in the ocean, tossing the aircraft carrier around. I could only imagine what it was doing to those LSTs. We'd go out and look and see the ship disappear as the bow went down into the water, then came back up. The hurricane was beating the daylights out of it.

Eye of the Storm

The ice from the sleet
would cut your skin

We finally made it through and went on to Mainland Japan to Mount Fuji.

We got to Mount Fuji in early October and were getting settled in. Mount Fuji is a dormant volcano, but they were snow skiing on the other side of it.

We lived in these things called Quonset huts. They were metal buildings with cement floors. Each hut had two kerosene heaters, one at the front door and one at the back door. We had about twenty-five Marines staying in these Quonset huts—about twelve on each side. We were just getting acclimated to it; it was starting to get cold. Then the hurricane hit Mount Fuji.

We went out and filled sand bags full of volcanic ash to stop the water from washing the volcanic ash that was already there from around the buildings where we were living. It got pretty bad out there. The rain came down with a mixture of sleet in it. If you turned your face to it, the ice from the sleet cut your skin.

I told the gunnery sergeant, "This is too dangerous, we've gotten into Storm Condition One, and it is too dangerous to stay out there and fill up those sand bags."

We went inside. One of my friends had been transferred to another platoon, in Communication. He said, "I'm going to go ahead and go on up there."

I said, "Man, why don't you just wait?"

With the storm as bad as it was, they weren't allowing anyone to go out on any liberty. I had taken off my rain gear and was sitting around with the guys. I was wearing a housecoat and some sweats, and I was telling the guys, "If this thing keeps storming like this, and it blows over one of these Quonset huts, we're going to have a major kerosene fire on our hands."

I was just making that statement, not hoping anything like that would actually come true. About thirty minutes later, this guy came bursting through the door. He was yelling, "Y'all get out of here! There's a kerosene fire headed this way!"

He obviously had been caught in the fire. When he ran through the fire, it burned his eyebrows off and burned off the first layer of his skin. Where the rain was hitting him, his skin was peeling off. It was like he had just one layer of skin left. You could see the blood running through his veins. That's how bad it was.

I ran everybody out of there. Whatever they had on, that's what they wore out of there. Some of them only had on a T-shirt and a pair of shorts. Some had shoes on, and I just had some shower shoes.

I cut off the kerosene heaters and ran out. We were out in the middle of the barracks area, and when I looked up I could see a large fire about the size of a building just rolling through. It was wiping out anything in its path. A lot of the Marines and civilians that were getting injured were caught in the Quonset huts. The windows were very small, so in order to get out of the hut, they had to run through the fire. If they were wearing a wet suit, it caught on fire. They were rolling around in the trenches, trying to put the fire out, but the trenches had the kerosene and the oil and fuel from the top of the base running into them, so the fire wasn't going out as fast as it needed to be. Initially, what they did was put huge fuel bladders at the top of the base and let the law of gravity send the fuel down to the base.

About my friend who had transferred to Communication, I asked him to just stay and wait until the next day, but he didn't. He just packed his stuff and went to the weapons company on the northern side of the base. He was blinded by the fire, and that just tore me apart. That was pretty rough.

We left that area and sat on the Japanese landing strip. They started pulling some of their planes out and letting us come inside their hub, for shelter—the majority of us didn't have anything on. I was wearing a housecoat, a pair of shorts, and some flip-flops. I ended up giving my housecoat to someone because he didn't have anything.

While we were sitting in there, they brought the first person in who had died. They brought him in on an Amtrak. That was pretty devastating.

They moved us into a little nightclub. In this nightclub, we were standing around in water about two feet deep. We had been standing in water so long that our feet were wrinkling up, and our skin was turning different colors.

The Japanese had a barracks across the street from us, and they put their people on liberty and allowed us to come over and spend the night. At least we had a warm place to stay, because this was during the winter. We were up there for cold-weather training, and we couldn't take a shower. We didn't have any clothes, but at least we were out of the elements.

We ate breakfast at the mess hall for the Japanese, and it was the first time I had ever seen barbecued salmon. They had little salmon in a can that they ate for breakfast, and they ate a lot of rice.

That night, they gave us a lot of sake and stuff like that, and the next day, we tried to loosen up. We played a little volleyball, and the general came down and interviewed a lot of us. He asked me, "What do you think?"

I said, "Sir, we need to get out of here."

He said, "If we leave and don't rebuild, no one will want to come back here. We are going to have to suck it up, rebuild, and stay here to prove to other companies that come here that it is safe to come here and train."

The following day, we salvaged everything we could get. A lot of supplies were burned, and the club and the cafeteria were burned, too. A lot of things got burned up.

They pretty much had to rebuild three-fourths of the base itself, so we went back and we were like labor people for cleanup and all of that. We got everything cleaned up and started rebuilding, then went back to training.

Friends in Combat

I had a friend from Philadelphia, and he drove tanks. I was like an Amtrak commander. I was in Headquarters Company, and mainly I acted as the company career planner, but I also did training with the infantry units. We went on a maneuver, and it was early in the morning when we left. It was dark, maybe four o'clock in the morning, and they had already mapped out the direction we were going. We were riding in the Amtrak, following this tank.

The tank basically fell into a hole—a gigantic hole. Some engineers had gone out after the tank commander had mapped out the plan, and they dug a big hole. The tank fell into it.

Before, I asked my friend about riding with his hatch up. He told me he had been in Vietnam, and he only rode with his hatch closed when he was in combat, and that he didn't normally ride with it closed during training.

He was decapitated. That was devastating This was a dark time in my career. I had seen quite a few of my friends get seriously injured or killed, and we weren't even in combat.

I moved on from there, and we went on liberty to Tokyo and Gotimba.

It was pretty fun after we got through all of the initial shock of completing our cold-weather training. The climax was when we had to walk with complete packs, all of our gear and weapons and everything, our helmets, two canteens of water, and a change of socks. We had to do what they call a CREST, a Combat Survival Readiness Evaluation Test. We had to walk twenty-five miles and in eight hours. We did five miles, then ten, then fifteen, then twenty to prepare us to do the twenty-five. Walking twenty-five miles is no joke.

We completed the test, and the next day over half of the battalion was wearing tennis shoes. The guys' feet hurt, and we had blisters. The general said, "I didn't know we had all these tennis players in my company."

Everybody laughed, but we weren't ashamed of putting on some tennis shoes because our feet were killing us. Our cold weather training was complete and we returned to Okinawa.

I was playing basketball in the gym in Camp Swab in Okinawa. I went up to dunk the ball, and a guy undercut me, and I came down and broke the bone that runs along my small toe. When I hit the floor, I heard something break, and before I could get my shoe off, my foot had swollen. That night, there wasn't anything I could do but keep it elevated.

It was swollen up really badly. I went to the clinic the next day, and they took an X-ray. The doctor said, "Yeah, it's broken, and you are going to have to let the swelling go down before we put a cast on."

When he was x-raying my foot, he dropped the big bolt that screwed onto the X-ray machine, and that thing *just* missed my foot. I told him, "You want to see a grown man cry? If that bolt had hit my foot, I would have been crying like a baby."

I was kind of hardheaded, because I am a person who always likes to be on the go. Lying in bed was just killing me. I would get up and walk around, and my foot would swell. Then at night, when I would lay down and have it elevated, it would go down to normal. It was scary.

As time progressed, I was getting better, and my unit, Golf Company, was going back on another float to the Philippines. I had been to the Philippines once before Okinawa, and I wanted to go back. I couldn't go because my foot was in a cast, and we couldn't deploy on a ship while we were on light duty.

I wanted to prove to them that I was okay to go, so I told the corpsman to cut off the cast. He said, "It isn't ready."

I said, "I don't care, man. You've got to cut this cast off, because I've got to make them think that I am okay." My foot hadn't healed.

He cut the cast off, and when he was cutting it off, it was hurting. I put a boot on and walked with a cane. Then, I tried walking without the cane to let them think that I was okay.

While we were waiting to deploy, I went on liberty on another base below us called Camp Hanson, and I spotted a guy that had done me an injustice two years prior when I was stationed in Charleston. I followed him.

Vengeance Is Mine

Everything came back to me as if it had just happened. While we were in Charleston, we had to do what they call fan fire, where we didn't really shoot to score, just to get familiar with the weapon. We shot different weapons, like the machine gun, and the M16 and the .45—weapons that we carried. We were shooting the M16, lying down in the prone position. This guy was a staff sergeant, an E-6, and I was an E-3, lance corporal. There were three of us lying on the ground, and he told us to aim and prepare to fire, then command fire.

When he said, "Prepare to fire," the guy next to me fired, and he came over and kicked me in the butt and said, "What are you doing firing?"

I did everything I could to keep from getting up and hurting him. As I was getting up, the Spirit told me "No, no, no."

We were standing in line to fire the machine gun because we had to do it one at a time, and the guys were ragging me. One guy said, "Boy, did you see the dust come from Waiters's butt when he kicked him?"

I confronted the SSGT and said, "Sir, I think you owe me an apology. You kicked me, and I hadn't done anything."

He said, "I'm not going to apologize for nothing."

I said, "You take your stripes off, I take mine off, and you and I will go in the woods, and the best man will come out."

He said, "I'm not going in the woods with you."

"That's the best way we can settle this. There won't be any rank. It will just be man-to-man, since you kicked me and don't want to apologize."

"Well, I 'm not apologizing."

"I ever see you in the fleet, I will get even with you one way or another."

After reliving that moment I decided to let the Lord handle it. "Vengeance is Mine," saith the Lord. And besides I was trying to get back on the ship and I was not going to let anything stupid like that hinder me.

I went back to the Philippines, and the monsoon season had kicked in. We were a battalion that had several companies, and we were doing a lot of training. Each company had a career planner.

The commanding officer of the four companies decided to get with each career planner and make just one career planner. Since we were a battalion that had several companies, we were designated a battalion landing team, and we needed only one career planner.

The commanding officers had a meeting and decided they would make me the battalion landing team career planner. I received quite a few different accolades with that, because a lot of people were trying to reenlist and be stationed in the Philippines.

I tried to tell those guys that the chances of getting stationed there were slim to none. I received an award for enlisting so many Marines. When we were going back to Okinawa, the guys convinced me to go to drill instructor school.

I was scheduled to go to drill instructor school in August. I was going to leave Okinawa in June, spend a month of vacation, and then I was going to go to the school. I had planned on visiting my relatives in L.A. and San Diego, my aunt in Buffalo, and my brothers in Washington, where my car was. I was going to pick up my car and drive to South Carolina to spend some time with my parents, and then go on to Parris Island. I had a pretty good plan mapped out on how to spend my thirty days.

The last day on liberty, we had to be back on the ship at six o'clock that evening. When we got back on the ship, one of the guys said, "Man, the commanding officer is looking for you."

I said, "What did I do? I haven't done anything wrong."

When the CO found me, he said, "I am sorry about this. I have an award I want to give you. I won't be giving it to you in front of everyone because Parris Island has changed your orders, and you need to be there ASAP. As soon as you can get from Okinawa over there."

I said, "What?"

He said, "Yeah, you've got five days to get to Parris Island."

I thought, *Oh my goodness, this is going to be rough.*

He said, "We are going to put you on a C-130 and fly you out tonight from the Philippines, then back to Okinawa, and you'll catch a flight out of Okinawa back to the States."

That's not an easy thing to do, especially on a short notice like that. I said, "I want my record books and everything." I made them go through the correct boxes and get my record books out, and I got on the helicopter and flew back from the Philippines to Okinawa.

Man Made

I got to Okinawa, and they mailed my check to the ship we were on.

I told the administrator clerk, "Well, I don't want you to mess my pay up, so I'm not going to worry about it." They sent it to my last station, but I had to leave before it got there.

I still had a little money saved, but I had bought a bunch of furniture, so I didn't have a lot. I had enough to try to get home. I got a flight stateside into L.A., but I needed to get to Washington, D.C. I had left my vehicle with my brother, Larry in Washington, D.C., and I could drive it to Parris Island. I was trying to get a flight to Washington from Okinawa, and it was a difficult task; I only had four days now to report.

So they the airlines said, "Look, we can get you to Chicago." And then I got a flight to Washington.

After getting to Washington, I thought my brothers had my car, but my brother, Larry, had some problems with some girl, and she had cut my tires. They had put some more tires on my car and taken it to South Carolina, where my father was keeping it.

My family didn't know I was coming, and they didn't know exactly what I was going to be able to drive back. They had this truck; they called it the "Red Baron." They said, "We were going to take the Red Baron down to father; we just hadn't had a chance to do it."

I asked them, "Will it make it?" It was an old Ford truck.

They said, "Yeah, it will make it."

I hadn't had any sleep. I had been in the air flying, but I jumped on the road anyway. Right outside of Virginia, this guy was thumbing. The Spirit told me to stop and pick him up. I asked him where he was going. He said he was going to Charlotte, so I said okay. We started riding, and I was struggling to stay awake because I had not had any rest.

I asked him if he had a driver's license. He said, "Yeah, I got a driver's license."

"Well, let me see."

He showed me his driver's license, and I let him drive. I went to sleep. He could have taken me to Timbuktu. He stopped, got gas, and kept rolling.

He got to Charlotte and woke me up and said, "I'm here. I appreciate the ride." I was about thirty-five miles outside of Lancaster.

I drove on home, got my car, and drove down to Parris Island. While I was checking into Parris Island, the drill school burned down—and it was next to the fire department.

The next day, the commanding officer of the drill instructor school said, "We know the school burned down, but you are all still going to have to graduate on time because we need drill instructors."

They used us as laborers for a week to modify the barracks we were going to be staying in. They put our rooms upstairs and put us two to a room where normally we would have one to a room. They put classrooms downstairs and the offices for the instructors. We did a lot of things outdoors. I graduated from DI school.

I hadn't had any leave, because I had flown from the Philippines to Okinawa, then from Okinawa back to the U.S. I traveled three days. When we went overseas and came back, we were supposed to get thirty days of leave. They told me to check into my company and take my thirty days leave.

I checked into my company. I graduated in the top twelve of the class—we called ourselves "the dirty dozen." The top twelve basically had a choice of where we wanted to go. A lot of people wanted to go to the Third Battalion. Parris Island was broken down into four different battalions.

I graduated as a recruit from Third Battalion, so I really didn't know that much about the other ones. Everyone wanted to go to Third, and I didn't know why, so I chose Third, too. Out of fifty-two, they only selected six of us to go to Third Battalion. Everyone else was sent to First and Second battalion. We had about six females, and they all went to Fourth Battalion, which was the Women's Marine Recruit Training. I checked in, took my thirty days leave, and took off to go home.

I was home for two days, and my mom said, "Parris Island called."

I said, "Parris Island called? They're going to cancel my leave." She said, "You just got here."

I said, "They are going to cancel it. I'm not going to call them today. I will call them tomorrow."

I called them the next day, and they said, "Your leave is cancelled. Be back tomorrow, ready to go."

So I checked in, and they give me my mission. Generally, it was three drill instructors, with the senior being like a father figure. He was the experienced instructor. He taught all the drills, and the recruits pretty much hated his guts. The third guy was the newest in the group, and senior instructor pretty much took him everywhere. The new guy taught some drills, but he didn't do as much as the Heavy Aid, the second in command or as much as the senior did.

Back then, we didn't have cell phones or anything like we have today. I don't think we had any pagers, either. If they told you your pickup is going to be two o'clock, that's all you knew. At school, they taught you all the basics, but they didn't teach you about pickups and stuff like that.

One of the drill instructors was Sgt. Hawkins. He was the Heavy Aid. The Heavy Aid did the pickup and stuff like that. They told us we would get a pickup at two o'clock, and Hawkins said he was going to get a haircut. Then, they came back and said our pickup was now at twelve o'clock instead of two o'clock.

Well Hawkins was nowhere to be found, so I had to do the pickup. I said, "They didn't teach us that."

So the senior drill instructor said, "Just teach them positions of attention."

I went in there and was scared to death. I didn't really know exactly what to do, because they had really never shown us that. I taught a position of attention.

I said, "Are we motivated?"

They said, "Yes, sir."

I said, again, "Are we motivated? All right, I am going to teach you the positions of attention."

I took one recruit and showed him a position of attention, and then I said, "Get in there and grab your sea bag and fall out on the yellow footprints."

When all was said and done, the command staff said, "That was great. That was the best I've ever seen."

I said, "Man, don't be putting me in spots like this."

The new drill instructor normally worked about three weeks before spending the night with the recruits. He woke them up and got them ready, took them to breakfast and stuff like that. What they called "forming"—getting them ready—took about three or four days, and then we went into training day one.

We went through our forming in two or three days and went to training day one, and the senior drill instructor said, "We think you're ready. You can start spending the night."

We had only been there three or four days with them. That night, I could hardly sleep. I was worried about oversleeping and stuff like that. I tossed and turned. I was up at three o'clock in the morning, got them up around five o'clock, went to breakfast, and came back and got everything squared away.

We were going to go out and do the Initial Strength Test. We went to take the test, and it required a mile and a half run.

We had to do a minimum of three pull-ups and a minimum of twenty-five sit-ups in two minutes. They did the pull-ups, they did the sit-ups, and then we were getting ready to do the mile and a half. The battalion company gunny decided to do something different. He gathered all 250 recruits.

He said to me, "I hear you are doing a good job. How do you feel?"

I said, "I feel great."

I was burned out because I hadn't slept all night. We had on shorts and boots because we didn't have to run the test, the recruits had to do it. They were wearing tennis shoes.

The gunny told the recruits, "We are going to try something new. Your goal for the first mile is to kiss Drill Sgt. Waiters."

I thought, *What?* He was using me almost like a rabbit. I couldn't believe he put me in that position, because if those recruits had beaten me, it was going to hurt me down the road in terms of my authority.

I ran the mile of my life. I ran the mile—in boots—in five minutes flat. One recruit passed me. He did it in 4:40, and then at the end, he told me he was the Louisiana state champion in the mile. I could have knocked him out.

The company gunny came over and said, "Man, I didn't know you could run that fast. They said you were fast."

I wanted to knock him out. I told him, "Don't you ever put me in a position like that again."

Training went well, and we progressed through the three phases. The first phase was forming, where I taught them how to drill, and they did a lot of classroom time. We were breaking them down physically and then building them back up.

During the second phase, they went to the rifle range and spent a week snapping in, then another week qualifying.

Once that was finished, they went into mess and maintenance. The recruit who shot the highest got to pick what he wanted: mess duty or maintenance duty.

Recruits also got a flag with their platoon when they started out. It was a yellow flag with first and second phase, but the highest shooting in the platoon got a red flag. The red flag was still in the second phase, but it was an accomplishment. It showed achievement.

When we got to the rifle range, they had primary marksmanship instructors. They were the ones who took over and taught how to shoot and practice. The drill instructors just took the recruits from point A to point B and didn't get involved in any of the shooting techniques. They let the instructors take care of that. Each instructor had three or four recruits.

When a drill instructor had duty, we would spend the whole day with the recruits, even put them in bed at night. When we got up the next morning, the next drill instructor would come in and relieve us. It gave us a couple days off.

For six weeks, the senior drill instructor, Staff Sgt. Urich, would finagle the schedule so that I would work every Sunday. This was his last platoon, and he was supposed to be doing the majority of the Sundays. On Sundays, the recruits went to church, and when they came back, we did fun things with them. Mainly, though, the seniors were supposed to go out and work with them on the drills for the final competition. His job was to work with them during that time frame.

This guy was having me go out and work with them on Sundays. I was single and the youngest drill sergeant at Parris Island. I was excited about the opportunity, and I really didn't care at the time.

One Wednesday at the rifle range, I had worked the whole day and night. Thursday morning, it was his turn to come in and relieve me. He came in, said he had to run and take care of some matters with his wife, and left. Eight o'clock rolled by, then nine o'clock, ten o'clock, twelve o'clock. For the whole day, he didn't show up. I thought he would be back that evening to take them to dinner, but evening came, and he still wasn't there. I took them to dinner.

At the end of the night, we did hygiene inspections and let them write letters home and stuff like that. I did the hygiene inspection.

I put them on free time and then counted them off. I had them count one, two, or three, and then put them in the rack, and they went to sleep. Sometimes, I had them sing the Marine Corp hymn, "Halls of Montezuma," or recite the Marine Corp motto. Then, I would tell them to adjust and go to sleep.

I was at the light switch when he walked in. He had been gone all day, meaning I had done two solid days of work. He said, "You need to be back here in the morning at five o'clock to take them to breakfast."

I thought, *He must be out of his mind. He's been gone all day. He didn't show up, and now he wants me to be back here at five o'clock. I don't think so.*

The next day, I didn't come back at five o'clock. I came back at the normal time I was supposed to be there, at eight o'clock. When I got back, he had written me up for disobeying an order. He said he had ordered me to be there at five o'clock, and I hadn't shown up. He had me listed as UA—unauthorized absence.

They brought me in and reviewed my record book. The senior told them I had been out of town on a weekend, and that I was visiting my girlfriend in Charleston, and stuff like that. I hadn't even been off the island in six weeks.

The gunnery sergeant was reading all this stuff to me, and I said, "Are you serious. Is this for real?"

He said, "Yeah."

I said, "I don't think so." I told him what had happened, that I had worked the night before, and that he had come in that morning and left again. I told him the senior didn't show back up until ten o'clock that night, and he told me to be back at five o'clock in the morning. "That's why I didn't show up. As far as me going to Charleston, I haven't seen any woman. I haven't seen my family in six weeks. I have worked every Sunday for six solid weeks."

The gunnery sergeant couldn't believe that the senior drill instructor had treated me that way. He told me to take the next couple days off. "Matter of fact, if you want to go home and visit your family, then you do that."

The senior went around telling everyone that I dropped a dime on him, that I was telling them how badly he had treated me and this and that, and that I should be considered a person that can't be trusted.

I went to him and said, "Let me tell you something. The only reason I am not requesting a transfer is because the recruits have more loyalty for me than they have for you. If it weren't for them, I would definitely be requesting a transfer out of here to another platoon. You and I don't have to like each other. You don't like me, and I don't like you. I am going to get through this platoon, and they'll graduate, and I won't have anything else to say to you."

The platoon graduated, and later on in my career I eventually met Sgt. Urich at a conference. He said, "Are you still cocky and everything?"

I said, "Well, that's on you."

I worked with several other senior drill instructors. The next was Staff Sgt. Cooley. Cooley had been to Vietnam a couple of times. He had been in the army and then in the Marines. Cooley was a little bit on the psychotic side, and his superiors were always trying to catch him doing something wrong. Cooley was always doing something a little eccentric.

Once, Cooley caught a recruit eating some chicken in the back of the chow hall, in the storage area, and he made him eat the bone. This recruit was a dignitary's son, and they put Cooley on warning—if he screwed up again they were going to relieve him.

Later, we were on mess and maintenance. We had done well on the rifle range. On maintenance duty, drill instructors worked a couple of days at a time and then got a few days off.

Cooley had been working, and when I came in he said "Man, don't worry about nothing. I've got them locked on. You don't even have to get up at four o'clock. I got the squad leader to wake up the twenty recruits and call for a van to pick them up."

I told him "Man, I don't like this."

He said, "Don't worry about it. I got it squared away."

"I don't know about that."

"I'm telling you, I've got them locked on."

That night, Cooley told the squad leader to take care of it because he had been getting up every day and doing it, which I didn't know. At about four o'clock, the squad leader came into the office, and I woke up. He picked up the phone and said, "My name is Staff Sgt. Cooley. I need a van to pick up twenty recruits from Third Battalion and take them to West Company."

When he walked out, I heard a voice say, "Come here, recruit."

I thought, *Oh, my God. There goes my career.* I jumped up. I think I got dressed faster than I have in my whole life.

I was standing at the door, listening to someone ask this recruit, "Have you done this before?"

He said, "This is my first time."

"Do you know what laws you have violated?"

He said "No, sir."

The guy said, "Well, I can get you for using a government phone. I can get you for impersonating a drill instructor in the United States Marine Corp." He was just naming everything the recruit had done wrong.

This guy was actually a depot inspector. We called them depot spies. They looked for violations that drill instructors had made, things they may have done to put recruits in jeopardy or hurt somebody. They were kind of like watchdogs over the whole battalion.

When he got through with the recruit, I stepped out and said, "Gunny, can I talk to you?"

He had this smirk on his face. He said, "Yeah, you can talk to me."

I told him what I knew, and he said, "I knew Cooley was doing this. I have been getting up every day at three o'clock to catch him, but I never could catch him. I finally caught him."

He didn't catch Cooley, though. He caught me. He said, "I tell you what .I will let it go, but you tell Cooley he owes me one."

Cooley told the other drill instructors, and they laughed about it, but I didn't think it was funny. When I saw Cooley, I said, "I'm not going to listen to you again. I am not going to put my job in jeopardy because you are here playing. If you want to take chances like that, you can, but I am not."

Not long after that, he sent a recruit out to get some matches. The recruit went out to Cooley's car, unlocked the door, and got the matches. On his way back in, one of the depot spies saw him and said, "What are you doing?"

He told them he was getting Staff Sgt. Cooley's matches, and that was it. They relieved Cooley for personal servitude. Drill instructors can't use a recruit for personal service, not even going out to the car to get something. It was small, but they still relieved him. They had a list of violations against him.

The Compassionate
Drill Instructor

Then, it was just the other drill instructor, Volgowide, and me. Volgowide decided he was the Heavy, and I was the junior guy.

He said, "This is what we are going to do. We are going to counsel and recycle six recruits." To recycle a recruit meant he was not quite cutting it in the current stage of training. A recruit would be recycled and then go into another platoon if he was lucky.

I said, "Well, you counsel one, and I will counsel the other. We will alternate, and then we will recycle."

I sent in the first recruit for Volgowide to counsel. Volgowide told him, "You have been doing a decent job, but you are not quite cutting the mustard, so we are going to be recycling you and sending you back. Hopefully things will work out for you."

The recruit jumped up and took off. He ran down the hall and went out the back door, down a dirt road. I ran in the office and said, "What happened?"

Volgowide caught up with the recruit and brought him back. I said, "Let me talk to him."

I asked the recruit, "Why did you take off and run like that?"

He said, "Senior Staff Sgt. Cooley told us that in third phase, if you get recycled, you do one of two things: commit suicide or go your way. Sir, I am not committing suicide."

We knew then we weren't recycling anyone. If that is what Cooley had told them, it had been embedded in their minds, and we were going to have a problem if we recycled anyone.

The company commander asked us if we had any recycles and we told them no. "You've got no one that you recycled?"

I said, "We don't have any recycles. Everybody is cutting the mustard."

The company commander said, "That's hard to believe." We finished with that platoon, and they all graduated.

The next platoon, I had another senior drill instructor who was a pretty good guy, Staff Sgt. Moltrey. He was young, a little bit older than I was, but he was moving up really fast. He taught me a lot of things I hadn't learned. Following the Marine Corps guideline, there were procedures I could use to enhance my drill instructor skills. Some of the drill instructors had the platoon doing things that were asking for trouble.

In a series, there are four platoons. In the series I was in at the time, a drill instructor from another platoon had the recruits exercising in the shower, and a recruit was injured.

If you put seventy recruits in the shower at the same time, something bad is bound to happen. They couldn't all fit in there, and one of the recruits hit the water shower fixture and got a knot on his head. After this happened, they were sweeping—inter-viewing—the platoon. They interviewed everyone. They did an inspection on the platoon and asked them what had happened, and all the recruits said nothing.

The investigators brought the recruits in twice and asked them what had happened. A couple of days later, a recruit slipped a note under the commander's door and told him they had been mountain climbing in the shower.

He called us back in and told us he was going to reopen the inspection. We all said, "You need to leave it alone. You have talked to them twice. Just let it go."

He said, "No, we are going to have to reopen it." When he did that, two more recruits came forward and made allegations on their drill instructor, that he had made them mountain climb in the shower. They had a name for recruits that snitch—alligators.

They relieved all three of the drill instructors, pending investigation. Upon completing the investigation, they court-martialed the drill instructor who had them mountain climbing in the shower.

This started a trickle-up effect. Because of the allegations made against the drill instructors, the drill instructors came forward against the series commander. One drill instructor told of an incident when we were on the rifle range. When we were on the rifle range, we had bagged lunches. A series commander made the series scribe—another name for secretary—eat nine boiled eggs. The commander bet on how many the scribe could eat, and he made him eat nine boiled eggs. That series commander was relieved of his duties when all that came out. It just became a big mess.

The assistant series commander, Captain Chestnut, came to me. He asked me, "What should I do?"

I said, "Well, it's called CYOA (cover your own asset) now." Everything was hitting the fan, and everyone was trying to figure out what to do.

I told him "If you haven't done anything wrong, just tell the truth." They ended up making him the series commander, and we ended up graduating. Those were some interesting times, my drill instructor days.

A Helping Hand

I was transferred to support battalion. The elements that made up this battalion included: receiving, casual, Marine Corps history instructors, swimming, hand-to-hand combat, dental liaison, and Marine liaison at the naval hospital. My first tour was in casual, where the recruits were awaiting discharge. This was a break from the drill field, after drill instructors had graduated three or four platoons. We got about a six-month break and then went back to the drill field. We could easily have burned out processing too many platoons back-to-back without a break. I was in casual for about six months. I saw the recruits coming in and going out.

The strangest case I had in casual was a recruit who had stolen a Corvette when he was younger. He took a joy ride in the Corvette, drove it around and parked it again. His wallet fell between the seat and the console, and he got caught. They arrested him, and he was sentenced. Somehow, he got in without those charges coming to light. Eventually, those charges did pop up, and they got him for fraudulent enlistment.

They asked me to take him to the legal office. When we came out of the legal office, sheriff deputies were waiting there to handcuff him.

He said, "I can't believe I am being turned in."

I said, "Man, you should have told the truth from the beginning, and they could have worked it out. You wouldn't be going through this."

There was another recruit whose name was Lewis. He looked like an older guy, but his record said he was twenty-two years old. I said, "Lewis, how old are you?"

"I am twenty-two, sir."

I said, "Man, either you've had the hardest life a twenty-two-year-old has ever had, or you aren't telling me the truth.

The day before he was discharged, they called and asked me if I had a Lewis Brown Johnson, alias, Wilson, and I told them I had a Lewis.

They said, "Well, he's a fraud. You need to take him up to legal services and see one of our attorneys."

I called him up. His last name was Brown, but he was using Lewis. I asked him what was going on, and he said he was living in New York and had assumed his cousin's identity. His cousin was twenty-two years old. He had used his cousin's name, Social Security number and date of birth. He was actually twenty-nine years old.

I asked him, "Why did you do it?"

He said he had a $250-a-day heroin habit. He knew the system in New York, and all they would do is put him on methadone, and he didn't want to do that. He wanted to kick the whole habit, and he felt like joining the Marines would be the best way to do that. There would be no way he could get a hold of any, and he wouldn't have to take the methadone. I asked him when he had used heroin last, and he said it was the day before he was shipped out. I also asked him about the withdrawals.

He said he had been having them, but there was so much drama going on, he was able to handle the withdrawals. He had been on the island for about two-and-a-half months, and he had basically kicked the habit.

I took him to legal, and they basically set him up for fraudulent identity. His cousin, whose identity he was using, got arrested in New York. He told the police someone was using his identity, because when they ran his statistics, they showed he was enlisted in the Marine Corps. He had to tell them his cousin in Parris Island was using his identity.

The third recruit I dealt with came to the island and refused to cut his hair or put on the uniform. They told him, "You are going to cut your hair and you are going to put the uniform on."

He said, "I'm not going to do it."

He had been in college for three years, and it was time for him to go to officer candidate school. In the meantime, he said his religion had changed, that he didn't want to fight and refused to go. He made it known that he was a conscious objector. They told me to take him down to see the Sergeant Major.

I took him, and he was cursing every step of the way. He called the Sergeant Major all kinds of names. He was cursing at him for everything he could think of. The funny thing was, they had a little memo going around the battalion stating that if a recruit was caught cursing, there would be a one-hundred-dollar fine for every curse word, so when the Sergeant Major was through with him, I said, "You owe me about $2,000."

The Sergeant Major told him to leave the office, tuck his head between his legs, and not look at his American flag.

I was talking to the kid on the way back, and I asked him, "What's your story?"

He said, "They think they are going to win, but they're not. Just wait and see. I am going to get out of this deal."

When we got back, there was a call waiting for him from the Secretary of the Navy. I don't know what the Secretary of the Navy said to him, but he got his haircut and he put on the uniform.

Shortly afterward, he typed a letter and submitted it to the headquarters of the Marine Corps. He was later discharged.

THE STRENGTH OF
THE FAMILY AND THE
PASSING OF THE BATON

I was dating my wife at the time, and we were making plans for our wedding in the spring.

My grandmother had already given me a blanket for our wedding gift, because, for some reason, she felt she might not be living when we got married.

The morning of our wedding, April 24, 1982, my grandmother died. My father wasn't able to come.

I was going to postpone it, but they said no. Family had come down that morning, and the wedding was that afternoon. My dad said, "Things happen. Don't postpone the wedding."

We went on with the wedding. At first, it was a little gloomy, but once the service started, everything turned out okay. It was a really beautiful military wedding.

My brother had arranged for us to go to Bermuda for our honeymoon. We were planning to leave in a couple of days, then head out for Bermuda, but the commanding officer of the support battalion called me and said, "We have a job available as the Marine liaison at the naval hospital. If you want it, you got it, but there is one catch. You have to cancel your leave and take the job."

That job was one of the greatest jobs in the Marine Corps. The Marine liaison basically handled sick Marines who were awaiting military discharge. They were too sick to be on the base and were waiting for the military board to review their cases and send them home. Also, recruits would come over to be seen by doctors during the day, and it was the liaison's job to get their appointment, go see the doctor with them, and watch them until they got on the bus to go back. If a serviceman was hurt and in the hospital, the liaison would help him get his mail, make arrangements for him, and give him a hand with whatever needed to be done.

In February of 1983, I organized a Black History Month program. I invited several gospel groups from the community in Beaufort County, and my family came down. My father came also, and we had a very nice program. It was the first time something like that had been done at the hospital.

Just before the program ended, my father stood up and said, "I want to sing a song. This might be my last time, and I might not be able to sing it ever again." So he started to sing a song entitled "Strengthen Me Where I'm Weak and Build Me up Where I'm Torn Down."

That was the last time my father performed. Even today, when my brother sings that song or I hear that song, I get very emotional. That song is really touching.

My father got sick at my house that same day. He wasn't doing well, so we decided to put him in the hospital.

A year prior, my father retired from his job. On March 22, 1982, the doctors had told him he wasn't going to live unless he got a new heart. This was February 1983. On March 22, one year from the day he retired, he passed away. My father and I had planned to open a business. We had built a building out of posts and board. My father was going to pump gas and do the odds and ends inside the convenience store, and this was going to be his job until he passed away. I remember he and I were sitting in the building one day, and my father said, "Well, we got a top on it. I think it will make it."

I didn't know it at the time, but my father knew his time was short, and he wanted to make sure that we made it happen. We completed the building and put the gas in. He got to sell the gas and everything.

D. Frank said some of the same things I was thinking. He said, "Dad was on top of everything."

The day of my wedding, when our grandmother died, D. Frank was trying to console Dad, but Dad was on top of things, he didn't let anything get him down. He kept his eyes on the prize. Dad was so focused on what he had to accomplish that he didn't tell any of us what the doctors had told him. He let us think he was okay, and while in some instances, he was okay, he was trying to reassure us. Dad kept things together all the while knowing his time wouldn't be long. He put us in a better financial position because God gave him wisdom in business.

I needed a new van, and we needed a truck, because we hauled pulpwood, and I made trips. We saw a new pulpwood truck, and my daddy told me, "Let me buy this thing."

I said, "Dad, you are not working."

He said, "Just let me get it."

I had a 1980 van. We traded it in, and I got a new 1982 Dodge van. We also got the pulpwood truck with everything on it. That truck was in my dad's name, and he took out insurance on everything so that, in the event something happened to him, it would be paid off.

We didn't owe anyone anything when my dad died. Every vehicle we bought was paid off. Dad already knew what the situation was; he just didn't tell us. He kept us in the dark. He gave us a fresh start. We didn't have any debt at the time. He had fixed the family business—Uncle Bud's Place—so that we didn't owe any money on it either.

When Dad died, it shook all of us to the core. It affected us so that we were like chickens with our heads cut off. Dad was gone, and we were devastated. All of us, each affected in our own way by the loss of our father, asked the Lord, "Why? When it seemed like we were finally getting things going the way they should be, You stepped in and took Dad."

D. Frank dealt with it his way, and I had to deal with it my way. So did the rest of my family.

I came home for the funeral and was seriously debating about getting out of the service. When I went to the funeral, I was walking down the aisle toward the casket, carrying my brother's daughter, who was about one and a half years old. I was walking down the aisle with her, and someone, I don't know who it was, took her out of my arms as I was walking up to the casket. It's a good thing they did, because by the time I was about a foot away from my father, I passed out. Before I knew it, I had fallen on the casket, but I remember bracing myself as I was falling.

When I fell, there was this force that came out of the casket. I experienced the same kind of force with my uncle when he was in the hospital. It went through my arms and lifted me up, and my father came to me and said, "I am fine. Don't cry anymore. Take care of the family."

After that, I couldn't cry anymore. I can remember standing in line before we went into the church, and one of my sisters said, "You have got to be strong, because you are the glue that is holding this family together. If you fall apart, we will fall apart."

I said, "Why are you putting all the pressure on me? That's too much pressure."

She said, "No, don't you fall apart."

When I touched the casket, and that force, that spirit, went through my arms, it just straightened me up, and I couldn't cry anymore.

It wasn't but a couple of months after that I found out I was going to be transferred to California. I thought I ought to get out of the service, go home, and see if I could make the family business work. They said the only way I could get out is if I signed a new contract to go into the Reserves. The military spent so much money on me, and it would have been a waste if I got out right then, so I signed a new contract on Reserve status, and I was stationed in Greenville, where the ammunition company was.

I moved home. I had purchased a three-bedroom mobile home when I was on the drill field, and the government moved the home and set it up for me. My father and I had already cleared off the land. I knew my next duty was going to be in California anyway, so we were just setting it up so we could rent it out when I wasn't there.

I started several business ventures once I moved back home and got settled. When I went out to get gas for the station, the old gas pumps had to be brought up to standard. They weren't even equipped to go over a dollar. I had to buy a special kit to put on the pumps so the price could go over a dollar, though at the time, gas was still less than a dollar.

I went to some friends of mine who had a service station, and I asked them if they knew anyone who had the equipment. They told me to go to this particular guy and that if I had cash, I could get everything I needed. I went to the guy. I had about $10,000 cash, and I got lights, pumps, tanks, and everything, but those pumps needed this kit. So I went to Amoco and asked them about the kit. They told me the kit cost thirty-five dollars and took about fifteen minutes to put in.

The man at Amoco asked me, "Who are you buying your gas from?"

I said, "I haven't decided that yet, I am just in the development stage—getting myself together."

He said, "Since you don't know who you are going to buy your gas from, I just don't have time to put the kit in."

I couldn't believe it. His gas was going to be the highest, and I needed to have gas that was competitive. I was in a market where my gas had to be cheaper.

I was on my way back home that same day, and I saw a guy working on a Mr. G's pump. There were several Mr. G's stores in the community. He was putting the kit on the Mr. G's pump, so I stopped and asked him how much the kit would cost. He said the same thing, around thirty-five dollars. I asked him where I could get them from, and he told me I could get them from Florence, South Carolina.

He gave me the address and told me, "When you pick up the parts, call me, and I will come out and put them in for you." I went to Florence, bought the kits, and called him the next day. He came the following day and put in the kits.

I asked him how much I owed him, and he said, "Just give me a beer. I hope you will be successful, and don't let anyone hold you back."

About a year later, in May of 1984, my wife told me that she was pregnant. I said, "Lord, I would like to have a son."

When we went to the hospital to do the preregistration, the nurse looked at my wife and said, "You are going to have a girl". We hadn't done a sonogram or anything. She just told us, "You are having a girl."

My wife had at least fifteen girl names that she was looking at. I told her, "You need to come up with some boy names, because you are having a boy."

She said, "You don't know what you are talking about."

I said, "I am telling you, if you don't have any boy names when my son is born, I am going to name him Junior."

She said, "He's not going to be a junior."

The nurse said, "She is carrying a little girl."

I said, "No, she is carrying a boy."

She said, "How do you know?"

"I asked the Lord to give me a son, and he told me I could have whatever my heart desired if I accepted it and believed it."

"I have been a nurse for over twenty-five years, and I know when a woman is carrying a boy and when she is carrying a girl. Your wife is carrying a girl."

My wife believed she was carrying a girl. When the time came, she called me and said, "I am going into labor."

I rushed her to the doctor's office. We got to the office, and her water broke, and he said, "You need to rush her to the hospital."

We went to the hospital. She was in labor for eight hours, screaming and going on. They came to inject her with a needle, and I almost passed out. My blood sugar had dropped because I hadn't had anything to eat. They told me I needed to go get some chocolate, put the gown on, and come into the delivery room. I left, ate a piece of chocolate, and went into the delivery room.

When they delivered the baby, the doctor said, "Congratulations, you have a little boy," and my son started peeing on the doctor.

I said, "I told you."

My wife said "Oh, no!"

Then the following year, we had a daughter. We went to the hospital, and I thought they were going to let me go in and do the paperwork and everything. It took eight hours the first time, so we jumped out of the car and took her in, and they put her in the wheelchair and wheeled her to the delivery room. I parked the car, came back inside, and rushed to get to the room.

As I was walking into the hospital, the doctor started walking toward me and said, "Are you Mr. Waiters? Congratulations. You have a beautiful baby girl."

I said, "What?" It happened so fast. Within four to five minutes, she had already had the baby.

Angel in the Desert

The Mysterious Five Dollars

From 1985 to 1986, I went to different schools in the Marine Corps, sold mutual funds, sold life insurance, ran the store, and drove van trips. I was doing all kinds of entrepreneurial things. In 1986, I went to Quantico, Virginia, several times, and I went to North Carolina and worked in the ammunition department.

In 1987, I went to California for six months and worked as a tactics instructor in the NCO (Non Commissioned Officer) School. D Frank decided that he would ride out there with me. It was just him and me driving a van out there. My sister, Irene, brought him down from Washington and met me in Virginia. I drove from South Carolina to North Carolina and into Virginia, and he drove to Tennessee, and then I drove to Oklahoma.

When we got through Oklahoma, we headed into the panhandle of Texas. When we got to the panhandle, we stopped at a gigantic truck stop where we could take showers and rest up.

Prior to stopping, we had been alternating driving. One would drive for about six hours, and then the other one would drive for six hours. When we got to the truck stop, it was D. Frank's turn to drive, so I got into the passenger seat to sleep.

When I woke up, I asked, "What part of New Mexico are we in?"

He looked at me and said, "We aren't in New Mexico. You looked so good sleeping that I went to sleep, too, and we didn't go anywhere."

We ate breakfast and got on the road, traveling to New Mexico. When we left, we got into a long stretch of desert. As far as we could see, it was just highway and desert. No trees, no bushes, or anything. Then, the van broke down.

We didn't know what was wrong. We had plenty of gas, because we had filled up where we ate breakfast. What we needed was a jump, so we both stood there, saying, "Lord, we need someone to come along and give us a jump."

We were parked on the side of the road, and as far as we could see looking forward maybe a mile or so was nothing but highway. We couldn't see anything but highway, and looking back, another stretch of highway. We figured our best chance was that someone would come from the place we had breakfast, so we looked back that way.

A short time after that, we both looked around, and to the front of us, a white Ford Ranger had pulled up. We both looked at him and said, "Wow, where did you come from?" We couldn't believe he was there; it was like he popped out of nowhere. A gentleman got out. He looked as though he were an Indian. He was dressed in all white—white pants, a white shirt, and a white straw hat. He had little blue ribbons around his shirt pocket.

He said, "I understand you all need a jump."

"Yes, sir, we do."

I ran back to the back of the van and got some jumper cables, opened up the hood to his truck, opened up the hood to the van, put the jumper cables on, and boom, the van started up.

D. Frank said to him, "What do I owe you?"

He said, "You don't owe me anything."

"Yeah, I need to give you something."

"I am telling you. You don't owe me anything."

D. Frank reached into his pocket, pulled out five dollars, and said, "Take this five dollars." The man stuck the five dollars in his pocket.

I grabbed the cables and closed the hood on the van. Both of our doors were open, and we walked around, got in the van and looked up. The truck was gone. It was impossible for that truck to get out of our sight that fast in the desert. We could see ahead of us for five miles.

D. Frank said to me, "Do you believe what we just saw? That was an angel in the desert."

I said, "If I hadn't been here and witnessed it, I wouldn't have believed it, but I just saw it happen."

We both couldn't believe it. We were utterly amazed that something like that actually happened to us.

We drove on and got to California with no more van problems. We didn't know what the problem was, but it was like it had been instantly fixed.

I took D. Frank to LAX, and he got on the plane. Later, D. Frank told me he met a lady who looked like she was afraid. She was scared to death. Coincidentally, his seat was next to hers, so he sat down with her. She said, "I have never flown before, and I don't know how I am going to get through this flight."

He said, "Oh, you'll be fine," and started talking to her, and she asked him if he was a minister.

He tells her, "Yes, ma'am. I am a pastor." He told her he was going back to Washington and that he had come to California with his brother. They started talking, and he grabbed her hand,

and they started praying. He told her that he had worked for Eastern Airlines for thirteen years.

Well the next thing they knew, they had taken off and were landing. She couldn't believe it. She said, "Wow, this is unreal. God sent you here. I can't believe it. You were an answer to my prayers, because I didn't know how I was going to get through this flight. I have got to give you something."

He told her, "No, ma'am. You don't owe me anything."

She said, "Yeah, I owe you something."

"No, ma'am. You don't owe me anything."

"Here, take this five dollars," and she put five dollars in his pocket.

When he got home, he called me and said, "Guess what happened to the five dollars? The five dollars came back." Later, he preached a sermon about the angel in the desert.

"Be careful how you entertain strangers, for some have entertained angels unaware" Hebrews 13: 2.

A Marine's
Dream Home

I had applied for several recruiting positions, and in 1987, positions opened, and the headquarters of the Marine Corps decided to send me to recruiting school. When I got out of school, HQMC gave me a choice of duty stations. I asked for Philadelphia, Washington, or maybe Jacksonville. They came back to me and said, "You have two options: Orlando or the Bronx."

This country boy wasn't going to work in the Bronx, so I chose Orlando. As planned, when I graduated from recruiting school, I went on to Orlando. I worked there as a Prior Service recruiter, but I operated out of Jacksonville. I was now commuting from Orlando to Jacksonville. I did that for a couple of years, and I was promoted to gunnery sergeant. Eventually, I moved into the supervisory position, where I stayed for three years. I was the area supervisor for the entire state of Florida and Puerto Rico. I had offices in Jacksonville, Tampa, Orlando, West Palm Beach, Miami and Puerto Rico. I was traveling all over the place, inspecting and conducting interviews. This was nothing short of a miracle to me.

MIRACLES

Miracles have been a part of my life, all of my life. There is no other explanation for the way some things have happened in my life. For instance, in 1990, I was stationed in Orlando as a Prior Service recruiter. In the military, everyone holds an MOS, which means Military Occupational Specialty.

My job was to recruit qualified applicants for the Marine Corps Reserves throughout the state of Florida, but I had several MOSs I had to fill. They had to be qualified with a specific rank. I was given a quota to fill on a monthly basis. I had filled all positions throughout Florida for one particular month, except one—0151, Administrative Clerk. I called everyone in the state of Florida who was qualified, and they all turned me down. I had never missed quota.

The command had gotten strict, and they wanted specific MOSs with particular ranks. All of the guys who fit the qualifications I was looking for did not want back in the 0151 MOS.

A lot of guys who went into administrative positions stayed there. Promotions didn't come very quickly in administration, so whenever an opportunity came to get out of it, they'd get out. I was able to switch some of them over to different fields, but then they became real sticklers about wanting individuals to have the same rank and MOS in any particular field. This made my job harder than it really was, but even with all of that, I was still doing pretty well.

But anyway, this particular November, I was doing pretty well, but I still had one slot that needed to be filled. I called all of the 0151s in the state of Florida, trying to get them to take this position, which had to be filled by a corporal. I called several hundred, and they all told me no, that they would take any other field but that one.

I understood what they were saying, but it wasn't resolving my problem. I needed a 0151 corporal who was willing to accept that position. It was on the twenty-ninth day; I had one day left. When I got home, I got down on my knees. I said, "Lord, I don't know how you can do it, but I need you to send me a 0151. I need him to be physically qualified. I need him to be mentally qualified and morally qualified. In other words, I need him to already have his physical in hand and not have gotten into any trouble with the police. I need him to be a corporal, and I need him to be willing to join the Marine Reserves in that position. I need this guy to come in tomorrow and be ready to join, or I'll miss my quota. It would be my first time ever missing my mission."

I came to work the next day, the thirtieth. I had called everybody I could call, and now I was just looking out the window in my office.

At about 10:30 a.m., a young man walked in carrying a briefcase. He walked past my office and into the administrative office. He told them he was looking for a recruiter.

They said, "You want to see Gunny Waiters. He's next door."

He came over and knocked on my door and said, "Hello Gunny Waiters. I'm Corporal Anderson, and I'm interested in joining the Marine Corps Reserves."

I said, "Well, come in, Corporal Anderson, and have a seat. What's your MOS?"

He said, "I'm a 0151."

Quite naturally, I was smiling from ear to ear.

I asked, "How long have you been out?"

He said, "I just got into town. I got out of Camp Lejeune, North Carolina, and just got back to town." I thought to myself, *Thank you Jesus! Thank you Jesus!*

He opened his briefcase, and he had everything. He had his physical, and he was already under contract because he had just gotten off of active duty. Starting in 1986, whenever anyone signed up for the military, they signed an eight-year contract. All I had to do was make a copy of his information and have him sign some paperwork, and he was pretty much done. I know this wasn't logical; this was a miracle.

I know how God can work miracles in life, and that was one of them.

This is another story about how the Lord performed a miracle for me. I am thoroughly convinced He works in mysterious ways.

My brother, Joe Ray, had two daughters who both joined the army. They graduated from boot camp in St. Louis. He went to St. Louis to see his oldest daughter, Jori, graduate, so when it was time for his second daughter, Shannon, to graduate from boot camp, he told her he would wait until she graduated from MOS school—also known as A-school. Not knowing where her A-school was going to be, he simply made an open promise.

She had an intelligence MOS, so her A-school was in Arizona. I told him that if her graduation fell on my seven days off, I'd ride out to Arizona with him. The Lord worked it out, and sure enough, her graduation fell on my seven days off.

We got the kids together—I had my son and daughter, and he had his son. We had my great-niece with us, and we took a few more of our nieces and nephews. They all went to Arizona with us.

When we got on the road, I said to myself, *I wonder what kind of miracle the Lord's going to work this time?*

We made half the trip and stopped to spend the night in Dallas. It was a little bit chilly. We checked into a hotel, and the kids wanted to go swimming, but it was really too cold for that. The clerk at the hotel said, "No, you don't really need to go swimming."

The next morning, I got up and went to the store next to the hotel. I got some ice for the cooler and oil for the van. I walked back from the store and put the ice in the cooler and the oil in the van. We went to eat at a Jack in the Box located across the street from the hotel. Once we got inside my daughter said, "Daddy, I need some money to pay for breakfast."

I reached in my pocket, and I didn't have my wallet. I remembered having it when I bought the ice at the store, so I ran across the street to the store. I looked around, but my wallet wasn't in there, so I walked back to the van. I looked all around but didn't see my wallet.

I went back to the convenience store and asked the lady running the register if anybody had turned in a wallet. She said no but told me that people were pretty nice there, that people usually turned in things they found. She told me that once, someone turned in a $5,000 diamond ring they had found.

I went back outside, and I was checking the grass, looking for my wallet. I didn't find it. I even looked in the trash can, and I still didn't find it.

My brother had already paid for everyone's breakfast. We kept looking, and I said, "Okay, my wallet is not here." I thought someone had picked up my wallet.

I told Joe that one of two things would happen: I said if a Christian found my wallet, I'd get it back, but if a nonbeliever found my wallet, I wasn't going to get it back. I had my military ID, my sheriff's office ID, two or three credit cards, 300 dollars in cash, and my badge in my wallet.

I was so upset with myself because I taught classes in which I told people not to carry all those things in their wallets or purses, because if they lost them, they'd lose everything. I was beating myself up, riding with my head down, upset with myself about how I lost my wallet.

As we were traveling, getting close to Albuquerque and El Paso, I decided I needed to stop to cancel my credit cards. Whoever had my wallet could have the money, if I could just get my military ID, my badge, and my bankcards.

We had reservations to stay on the military base once we got to Arizona, so I really needed my military ID to get on the base.

I was riding along, feeling awful, and not paying attention to any of the scenery. We were supposed to be sightseeing, admiring the different terrain and enjoying the trip.

My great-niece, C.J., said, "Uncle Kevan, can I use your phone to call my momma?" I handed her my phone.

She was talking to her mother when she said, "They found Uncle Kevan's wallet."

I said, "They did what?"

She said, "They found Uncle Kevan's wallet."

"Let me speak to your mother."

"Uncle Kevan, they found your wallet. They talked to Grand-momma, and she has the gentleman's number."

I told my brother to pull over because I didn't want to lose the cell phone signal. I called my mother and asked what had happened.

She said, "This young man called from Dallas. He told me he had found your wallet. He was trying to get in touch with you so he could get it back to you."

In my wallet, I had three names and numbers on a yellow piece of paper. I had the number of an old roommate of mine from back in the '70s, Keith Marshall. I had my cousin's name, Wayne Coleman, and my number in there. Wayne lives in Wilmington, North Carolina. He's a retired Vietnam veteran. The man picked Wayne's number, called him, and asked if he knew Kevan Waiters.

Wayne said, "Yeah, that's my first cousin."

He said, "Well, I found his wallet in Dallas. Do you know how I can get in touch with him?"

"Sure, I can give you his mother's number, because Kevan's traveling and won't be at home."

He gave him my mother's number, and the guy called my mother. He gave her his number for me to call him.

I called him, and he said to me, "I'll bet you don't even know what the scenery looks like." I laughed because what he said was true. I'll bet you're riding with your head down, and you're beating yourself up about losing your wallet, aren't you?"

I couldn't do anything but laugh, because what he was saying was exactly the way I was responding.

He said, "I don't think the sheriff would be too happy about you losing your badge, and you're a master gunnery sergeant in the Marines!" He was just letting me have it, but in a fun way. "What do you want me to do?"

I said, "Just hold onto it, and I will get it when we come back through Dallas. I'll meet with you."

He said, "Okay, that's fine."

We went to Arizona, and my daughter Keri happened to have her military ID, so we used her ID to get on the base and get the rooms.

After we left Arizona, we met the gentleman who found my wallet in Dallas. He wouldn't take any money or anything.

The ironic thing is that he was a former Marine. He and his brother were on their way to do therapy at the VA hospital in Dallas when he saw my wallet. It had fallen out by the gas pumps when I walked by them. He was running late, so he just picked it up and went on. He didn't trust anybody with it. After he looked in it and saw I was a Marine and a deputy sheriff, he did a little research and found out how to get in touch with me.

They were very good people. I was just glad he was Christian and a Marine. I was glad I was able to get my wallet back.

From then on, when I go on a trip of any long distance, I don't make any smart remarks or statements to the Lord, like, "What kind of miracle are you going to work this time to show me how good You are?"

The Lord has shown me He can work miracles in my life, so I won't be running my mouth like that anymore.

I was stationed in Orlando from 1988 to 1993. In mid-1991, I received a phone call from a lady named Miss Tiller. Miss Tiller said she needed a huge favor from the Marines. I said, "Yes, ma'am. What is it?"

She said, "I would like to know if you and your staff would put your Marine dress blues on and say happy birthday to my son."

I said, "Sure."

She said, "Let me explain what happened. My son's name is Jacob Moseley, and at seven years of age, he was diagnosed with muscular dystrophy. He is fourteen years old now, and he will soon be turning fifteen. My promise to him for his sixteenth birthday is to give him a limousine ride around Orlando." She went on to tell me his life expectancy was eighteen. "He said something to me tonight that floored me, and I don't know what to do."

I said, "What did he say to you?"

"He told me he wanted to be a Marine, and if he couldn't be a Marine, he didn't want to live anymore. Instead of giving him the limousine ride at sixteen, I am going to do it now, at fifteen, because his birthday is coming up in August. Would you and your staff consider putting on your dress blues and telling him happy birthday?"

I said, "Sure, we can do that."

She called me back a couple of times and asked, "Are you sure you are going to do it?"

I said "Yes, we will do it," and asked her, "What does he like?"

She said, "He likes the Harrier airplanes. He wants to be a Harrier pilot."

I got a Harrier poster, and I got all the Marines in the unit to sign it. I put it in a frame, and I was going to present it to him for his birthday.

This was right after Desert Storm and Desert Shield, and we had a lot of memorabilia. The Marines were preparing things to give Jacob. We planned for one of the Marines to give him a hat and one to give him a cup. We also had a T-shirt for him. We had all sorts of things to give him for his birthday.

So the day came, and the limousine driver pulled up with Jacob and his friends to my office door. She got out and said, "I don't have his wheelchair, but I understand you are going to say happy birthday to him."

I opened the door to the limousine. I was standing there with my dress blues, and everything was looking really sharp. I said, "Jacob, I am Gunnery Sgt. Waiters, and I want to wish you a happy birthday," and I gave him the Harrier poster.

The look in his eyes, the glitter in his eyes was so refreshing to see someone that happy. He was so astounded. He didn't know this was going to happen. All he could say was, "Wow."

I said, "Jacob."

"Wow." He was just speechless. He couldn't say anything. I felt really good about it.

I stepped over, and the other Marines stepped up.

"I am Staff Sgt. Kemp, and I want to wish you a happy birthday," and Kemp handed him a cup. Then another Marine handed him a T-shirt.

We felt really good about it. Miss Tiller, Jacob's mother, wrote a letter to the editor of the Orlando newspaper and called it a "Marine's Dream." She gave a brief synopsis of her son's desire to be a Marine and the request she made for his birthday. She wrote about how she had met some outstanding Marines who helped carry out her birthday wish for her son. She stated that she had never seen her son that happy.

I thought it was a pretty nice article. During this time, there was a United Airlines pilot in town who was a former captain in the Marine Corps. He read the article in the newspaper, called me up and said, "Gunnery Waiters?"

I said "Yes, sir."

He said, "I had the same dream that young Jacob Moseley had, and when I grew up, I became a Harrier pilot for the
Marines. I stayed in the Marine Corps for eight years. I got out
as a captain, and now I am an airline pilot for United Airlines. I
have a Harrier plane that I built that I would like for you to present to Jacob for me."

I said, "Sure, I will do that. When can I pick it up?"

He said, "No, I live in Philadelphia, but the plane is at my parents' house in Pittsburgh, where I grew up." He said that when he
got back into that area, he would put it together and mail it to me.

I told the other Marines about it, and they said, "Oh, that
officer is not going to send that plane. He is just pulling your leg."

I said, "No, he is going to send it. If he wasn't serious about it,
he wouldn't have mentioned it to me."

Sure enough, three weeks went by, and we received a gigantic
box. I opened it up, and there was this beautiful Harrier airplane
inside a glass case. I knew that thing was worth several thousand dollars. I went to the mall and had a nameplate made with
the name of the captain on it and an inscription that read: Presented to Jacob Moseley. I placed it under the nose of the plane. I
brought it back, and I told his mother, "I want you to bring Jacob
over. I have something I want to give him."

When I was a drill instructor, my unit had given me an
American flag. It was very sentimental and personal to me. I
knew this plane had to be super personal for that captain, and if
he was willing to part with that plane, I could part with that flag.
I folded the flag and put it in a nice display.

When he came over I said, "Jacob, I have something I want
to give you," and I gave him the plane. He was blown away by it.
Also, I presented him with the American flag. I told him that it
came from the unit. I didn't tell him it was my personal flag.

After that, Miss Tiller wrote another letter to the editor and
the newspaper came to interview me. They asked me how we got

involved, and they asked about the history behind the plane and the flag. I told them the flag was my personal flag.

When they wrote the article, Jacob read it, and he called me and said, "Sarge, I didn't know that was your personal flag."

I said "Yeah."

His mom said that when they were on their way home after I gave him the plane and the flag, he told her, "I know I don't have long to live, but when I die, I want to be buried in this flag."

She said she just cried all the way home. When she told me that story, I started thinking. One of my co-workers, Gunnery Sergeant John Bailey, was a pretty good writer. I said, "Let's do this—let's write a letter to the Commandant of the Marine Corps and see if we can make Jacob an honorary Marine."

Sure enough, we wrote the letter, and they sent us a reply. The Commandant made Jacob and another young man in Ohio honorary Marines. The other young man was in their delayed-entry program. He was in a diving contest and broke his neck, and he was paralyzed from the neck down.

So they made Jacob and him the first-ever honorary Marines. As more people heard about it, they really wanted to get involved. Miss Tiller said, "I want to give him a ceremony. This may be the biggest event in his life. I may never get to see him graduate."

My commanding officer from Atlanta wanted to present the Honorary Marine Certificate to him.

I said, "Great. Let's get him a set of dress blues."

They said, "We'll give him a set of cammies."

I said, "Any kid can get a set of cammies. We need dress blues."

They said, "Those things cost $300 to $400."

"So?" I said, "That's okay." I started calling in favors from Marines around the country who owed me favors. I said, "I need you to buy a hat. I need you to buy shoes. I need you to buy trousers." We put together a set of dress blues. I asked Miss Tiller for his sizes.

She said, "What do you need that for?"

I told her "Don't worry, just give me his sizes. Jacket size, shoe size, and stuff like that."

We got him a set of dress blues and set up a ceremony date. They made a big cake with the Marine Corp emblem on it and "Honorary Marine Jacob Moseley" written on it. We had all the Marines from the Reserve Center truck company in Orlando at the ceremony and also the Navy Reserve Unit. We had another Marine who had been awarded a purple heart in Vietnam but had never received it. He was an older gentleman. They wanted to know if he could be a part of Jacobs's ceremony so they could present him the Purple Heart. I said, "That's great."

We had TV coverage from *Headline News,* CNN, and the local news stations from Orlando. This ceremony was growing into a large event. It had nationwide media coverage.

During the ceremony, when they called Jacob up, I presented him with a mounted safari hat that the PMIs used on the rifle range. I had the hat put on a plaque, along with a poem I had written for Jacob. The plaque had the Marine Corps emblem on it. The Marine Corp League also presented Jacob some gifts.

When it was time to make Jacob an Honorary Marine, I rolled him out in his wheelchair, and they made him one of the first honorary Marines. Everybody had a really good time.

There was some crazy guy there. No one knew him. He invited himself to the ceremony, and afterward, he wanted to go with Jacob's family to dinner. They thought he was a friend of mine, and I thought he was a friend of theirs. We soon discovered he wasn't either of our friends. Later, Miss Tiller told me this guy started calling Jacob and asking him crazy stuff. I told her to give me his number and that I would take care of him. I called him up and said, "If you ever call Jacob again, you will have to answer to me," and that put an end to that.

More articles were in the newspaper about the event. An actual Harrier pilot, a major, flew down to Orlando in a Harrier plane. He told me he was looking for Jacob, and I told him where he lived. He went there, picked him up, and put Jacob in the actual plane. He gave Jacob a jump suit and a call sign—"Devil Pup." It was just beautiful.

The Marine Corp Ball was coming up, and I told Jacob he would go as the youngest marine. As a tradition, the youngest Marine and the oldest Marine cut the cake, and the youngest one feeds the oldest one a piece of the cake. I told Jacob, "Since you are going to be the youngest Marine at the ball, you will be cutting the cake along with the oldest marine."

We had the Marine Corp Ball in November 1992 at Sea World in Orlando, and it was beautiful. The ballroom had wall-to-wall red carpet. We had a fifty-piece orchestra, and everything was immaculate. We wheeled Jacob over, and Jacob and the oldest marine cut the cake together, and the youngest marine fed the oldest marine a piece of the cake.

I tried to keep Jacob motivated. Whenever I learned Jacob was slacking in his grades, I would call him up and say, "Jacob, let's get it together. Marines don't be failing." I tried to give him motivational drive. Jacob graduated from high school.

He wanted to meet the basketball player, Shaquille O'Neal, from the Orlando Magic. I took him to the Magic games. I had season tickets, so every time I had an opportunity to go, I took Jacob with me. We went to a couple of games. My children were still young, and I would bring them with me, too, and we would do different things with Jacob. I would go by and talk to him and just have a good time with him. When I moved from Orlando to Daytona, then from Daytona to South Carolina, I stayed in touch with him.

In 2006, I called to check on Jacob and found out Jacob had passed the year prior. They buried him on July 25, 2005—my birthday. In August 2006, I went back to Orlando to arrange a memorial service for Jacob, to honor him as one of the first honorary Marines.

In 1993, I left Orlando and was transferred to Daytona Beach. I was transferred to the recruiting sub station there as the NCOIC—the non-commissioned officer in charge of that recruiting station. I was promoted to E-9, Master Gunnery Sergeant. In this position, I had several recruiters who worked under my command, covering east central Florida. We recruited from sixteen high schools, four colleges, and two universities. I basically floated around to different areas and taught different recruiting techniques. I also trained my guys on a regular basis once they got out of school.

During my tour in Daytona from 1993 to 1996, I was instrumental in helping one of the areas in Daytona where there were a lot of single mothers with children. We staged events in the neighborhood to give the mothers and children some hope.

It was a predominately-black neighborhood, and the mothers were young. Anything to help advance the children was needed. I was able to bring in the Silent Drill Team, a very prestigious unit, which performed all over the world. That really gave the community a boost. The community was situated near Bethune-Cookman University, and we were able to do some recruiting from that area also.

I was asked to speak during a program honoring five of the Tuskegee Airmen. I was asked to write a poem for them, and I didn't know what to do. These guys had so many credentials and accomplishments, I felt honored to even stand in the same room with them.

The program was held at Daytona Beach Community College. In attendance for the program was the president of the college, the mayor, and other distinguished community officials. They each had words of acknowledgement and presentations for the Airmen. The Airmen spoke of their experiences in college, flight school, and in battle. All of their accomplishments and adversities were compiled in a book that we now know as: *The Tuskegee Airmen*. After all of them had spoken, it was my turn. I was bringing up the rear.

The Lord had lain on my heart to write a poem about the five Airmen, so that is what I did. I broke down the importance of what they had done. They were so excited about it.

At the end, I tried to get their autographs, and they told me they wanted my autograph. We all had a good time. It turned out to be a really nice program.

When I left Daytona, I was torn between staying in the service and getting out, and I had an opportunity to go to three different duty stations: Houston, Sacramento, or Detroit.

I had been in a warm climate for over ten years, so I said no to Detroit, because I know how cold it gets there. In Sacramento, it rains a lot, so I wasn't too crazy about it. I had a friend that was running everything in Houston, so I went to Houston, and they laid out the red carpet for me and said I was going to be working in Galveston. It was similar to the Daytona Beach climate. They really made it interesting for me, but when I got back on the plane, the Lord just told me I was done.

I wasn't happy anymore like I used to be about it, when the kids were the inspiration for me. It was getting to be very political, so I decided I would move on.

COMING HOME AT LAST

In the meantime, I was building a boot camp program. The Volusia County Sheriff Department had built a million-dollar building to house juveniles in this boot camp program. These kids were on the verge of being career criminals, and they had an opportunity in this boot camp program. They asked me to put together a curriculum to teach their deputies to be drill instructors. I went to Parris Island and got the updated manual, and I combined their concept with the boot camp program they already had in place and added my ideas. For two weeks, I taught them how to teach drill, how to get them into the shower, how to make them get on line, and how to make a rack.

They were so impressed that they offered me a position when I was ready to retire. I considered it, but I decided if I was going to do anything, I preferred working in law enforcement back in my hometown.

I came home and put in an application with the Lancaster County Sheriff Department. I put in my application, had an interview with the sheriff, and got hired the same day.

He told me, "Don't go look for another job. You're hired. You will be able to start in a couple of months."

At the beginning of 1997, I went to the South Carolina Police Academy in Columbia, rated third in the nation. Upon graduating from the academy, the sheriff's office sent me to School Resource Officers' training in Tampa, Florida.

When I graduated from School Resource Officers' training, I was sent back to Columbia to attend Crime Prevention School. After graduating from Crime Prevention School, I was sent to Charlotte, where I attended and graduated from Bike Patrol School. Having completed all the schooling and training, I made another giant step in my career—I became the first ever black detective in the history of the Lancaster County Sheriff's Office. I worked in the detective division for four years. During these four years, I had the life-changing experience that convinced me to write this book. After my time in the detective division, I worked on the street as a shift patrol supervisor.

In addition to working at the Sheriff's Office, I was trying to get my business back up to par. I got my children in school, and they were doing well. My son was playing football for South Middle School, and they needed a coach. My son played offense, and I started coaching defense. My nephew was playing defense.

Brandon won the academic award for the football team. I was really proud of him. It wasn't just his performance on the field, but in the classroom, also.

My daughter, Keri, was valedictorian of her elementary school. She wrote her acceptance speech for the award. When we watch the video of her speech, it brings us to tears.

THE FIGHT IS ON

D FRANK

We used to sing this song with the lyrics, "*I'm fighting for my life/ If anybody asks you what's the matter with me/Tell them I'm saved, sanctified, Holy Ghost-filled, fire baptized/I've got Jesus on my side, and I'm fighting for my life.*"

No one could have told me I would be in the fight of my life. When I realized there was a problem in my body, I went to the doctor. In 1995, I went to the Veterans hospital to have tests run on my eyes, because my vision was giving me a problem. After several checks, I was informed I was a borderline diabetic.

Immediately, they started me on medication. The meds they gave me worked for one condition but wreaked havoc in other areas. They started causing kidney failure. After about a week of taking the meds, the doctor informed me my creatinine level had gone from 1.5 to 2.6. I didn't know if that was good or bad; I just accepted what he told me. He said I needed to start taking insulin, but I refused to take insulin. He told me that without insulin, my condition was worsening.

Little did I know, my condition was worsening because of the medicine they were giving me. Less than two years from the first time I used the medicine, I had complete renal failure. I knew they were trying to help me, but they were not listening to me.

I would always ask questions. I wanted to know why they were giving me certain meds, what their purpose was. I soon found out I also had congestive heart failure. I was already having problem with my eyes; things just started falling apart. My perception of the health care I was receiving grew very distorted. It seemed like everything was going too fast—my house of cards was falling down from 1995 to 1997.

I received encouraging words from family and friends to stay the course and not give up. I heard in a small voice these words: *Whatever you're going through, I will bring you out.* I stayed the course, and God blessed me. Before it was all said and done, I went through several ordeals, but I had the word from the Lord that He would bring me out.

It was hard sometimes, but God was better to me than I was to myself. I had to go on dialysis to have my blood purified and returned to the veins. Then, there was another procedure a little different from regular dialysis that I could do at home. I opted to do that procedure. My doctors had varying opinions about that. One doctor told me I would be a successful candidate, and another told me I wouldn't be a good candidate. His prognosis was that I should continue with regular dialysis, meaning I would have to sit three or four hours a day, three days a week. I hated that with a passion, but I resolved that if that's what I had to do, then so be it.

The process became easier after I accepted that it was going to be my path. I had this condition, and I was going to have to live with it. I didn't even get on the list for a kidney transplant, initially. My mindset was that I could handle it, so I signed up for the home treatment dialysis. That way, I could travel, preach, and still do some things that I wanted to do. It was my way of being in control of the situation. However, there was a downside to home treatment—I was more susceptible to infection. The area had to be sterile and private. Contracting any type of infection would cause me to lose the ability to treat myself.

In 1999, I had continual hospital visits, either due to infections or to my body simply messing up on me. It became apparent that clinical dialysis or home treatment dialysis would no longer sustain my life. I was faced with dire consequences; I needed a kidney transplant sooner rather than later. The doctor told me I would be okay for a few years on dialysis but not to expect any longevity. He told me, "I'm not saying you are going to die tomorrow, but I am saying you need a kidney transplant." I told my doctor I hadn't even considered that.

I told him also how many brothers and sisters I had, and he said, "I'll bet you, if you have that many siblings, somebody's going to match up with you, and it will be a good match."

My sister, Denise, heard the doctor and she said, "Well, brother, I'll give you a kidney."

The severity of this situation hit me hard. Last time I was in the hospital, I didn't know I was alive for five or six days. Doctors told me they nearly lost me a couple of times due to my condition.

After Denise offered to give me a kidney, the doctor said, "Well, that would be good, but it would be better if you had a male kidney." My oldest brother was a diabetic, so that left my three brothers in South Carolina. I called all of them and asked, and they all said, "Yes."

In June 1999, they were all tested. All of them were compatible, but Kevan was a perfect match. It was like his kidneys and mine were the same. We decided that Kevan would be the donor. The fight was on. I had a donor, but I was sick. I was in no condition to receive the kidney. I was one sick puppy.

I was also facing economic disaster. I wasn't making any money; I had no money coming in. The doctors at Washington Hospital Center told me they couldn't do the transplant, because I would be unable to pay for the medicines I would need.

They wouldn't do it. One of the doctors asked if I had been to the Veterans Administration. I told him, "No, I didn't know the VA did transplants."

He told me they did them at Walter Reed, the army hospital. I went to the VA renal clinic, and they told me transplants were only done for active duty personnel, not veterans. They advised me to check with the National Institute of Health and even put me in touch with a contact person. I talked with a lady at NIH to see if I fit one of their profiles to receive a transplant. I did fit one of their protocols; I already had a donor, and he was a perfect match. They were eager to do it.

I believe it was the Lord's intervention that allowed this to come to pass. I didn't have any money. The NIH would allow me to get the transplant, and they would even provide the medicine I need to sustain it. Things got underway pretty quickly, but there was still one major problem—I wasn't well.

Dr. Kirk and his team of doctors advised me that before he could perform a transplant, I had to be well enough to accept it. He wasn't putting a good kidney into my body to kill it. We set on a course to get me into condition to accept a transplant.

We were scheduled to have it done in December of 1999, but I wasn't ready. They moved it back to January of 2000, but in January, I wasn't ready. They moved it to February, and I still wasn't ready. I ended up having knee surgery in February, and that kept me from having the transplant.

I was getting angry. I wanted to get on with my life. I hated going to dialysis. I was fighting with the VA for benefits. They kept denying me, stating I didn't have justification for filing. It was a nightmare that seemed like it would never end. I was in a mess. I reached a breaking point, and I told my doctor, "I am tired. Every time I come for the transplant, you tell me we can't do it for this reason or that reason. The next time I come, either give me the transplant, or I won't be coming back anymore."

In April of 2000, my surgery was scheduled for the fourth time. I had received clearance to have the operation. I went to dialysis for the last time on the morning of April 1, 2000. I had already declared, "One day, when I come to this clinic, it will be my last day, and I will never have to come in here again." This was that day. It had finally come.

We checked in to the hospital on the third of April, and the transplant was to be done on the fourth. All systems were go; we were all doing our thing. It was getting pretty close. They said they were going to come and prep us. My brother would be going down first and while they were operating on him they'd bring me down and have me ready so they could put the kidney in. Well, the Tuesday morning we were ready. Then they call me up and tell me, "There is a problem".

The Call

I come to you at a place and time in my life when things have finally begun to settle down. I returned to my home in South Carolina from my stint in the military, though I am still on active reserve status. I was blessed to have seen places some will perhaps never see. I traveled to some of the world's most remote places, so remote, that I was told; "The further you go in any particular direction, and you will see human beings that we know as head hunters and cannibals". Suffice it to say, I didn't go any further.

The military afforded me opportunities that I may not have gotten otherwise, but I have always been a hard worker,—so maybe I would have. From my youth, our father instilled values and morals in each of his children, and with his instruction, we had the tools and headed out in the right direction.

I moved back to Lancaster, South Carolina, to be near my mother. She was getting on in age, and I want to be close by so that whatever she needs, she will have it. I'm doing pretty well, no complaints. I'm back home near mother, working as a detective at the Lancaster County Sheriff's Office, and going back and forth to Greenville, S.C., doing my reserve work. Life was good.

Then I got this phone call—"Brother, will you give me ... ?"— and another chapter of my life began. Knowing the love my mother has for all her children, and the fact that she had already lost one son, my mother's humble beginning, and what she and her family endured to protect the children and the livelihood of us all, it wasn't even an issue. I didn't even have to think about it: The answer was, "Yes."

In 1999, I received a call from my brother, D. Frank. He had been sick on and off, on dialysis probably about four or five years. I was going to Washington periodically for his dialysis. He was on dialysis three days a week: Tuesday, Thursday, and Saturday. He would be just burned out when he was finished with the treatment. In 1999, he called three of his brothers, who were all living in South Carolina—Larry, Joe, and me.

He called me at home and said, "I need to ask you a favor."

I said, "What's that?"

"Would you consider donating me a kidney?"

"Sure, that's no problem." When I hung up the phone, I really didn't know the significance behind being a donor. I just knew I was willing to do it. Later, the Spirit came to me and said, "You're the donor," but honestly, even at that point, I really didn't think that much of it.

The three of us went up to Carolinas Medical Center in Charlotte, where we each took a blood test to see which one of us was a match.

About a week later, they called, and they were jumping up and down, and they said, "All three of you are a match, but Lieutenant, you are a perfect match. We want your kidney."

Initially, the transplant procedure was to be done at a hospital in Washington, DC. Medicare was going to pay eighty percent of it, and my brother was going to have to pay the other twenty percent. Because the medication was so expensive, the same eighty-twenty payment plan was going to be used. However, his medication was going to run roughly $3,000 a month, meaning his twenty percent was going to be $800 a month.

He said, "Wow, $800 a month is a lot of money. That's a house payment."

I said, "What about checking with the Veterans Administration to see if they would pay the other twenty percent?" He had gotten so sick that another one of my brothers and my mother went up to see him. My mother said the Spirit told her to go up and see him. He had just dropped down.

My other brother, Larry, said, "You don't want to see him. He looks really bad." My mother told him that he needed to get out of the hospital because God wasn't through with him yet.

He was still having medical problems, and we were trying to arrange the transplant. I told him, "What you need to do is go to the VA to see if they will pay the twenty percent." He did speak with a woman from the VA, and she told him they would do it.

Because I spent twenty-four years in the military, I said, "Whoa, wait a minute." We were at a very pivotal point in my brother's life, and I needed assurance in writing of what my brother had been told.

I was still doing consulting work in Greenville. I was working at the sheriff's department, and once a month, I was going to Greenville to work. Along with the consultant work, I was scheduled to go to Colorado that following summer.

With all this in place, my brother asked, "Would you consider donating me a kidney?"

When they determined I was a perfect match, and told me he spoke to someone at the VA who told him they would do it, you better believe I said, "I want to see this in writing."

I went to the VA in Washington and said, "I want to talk to the person who talked to my brother, who said they would make up the 20 percent."

The nurse said, "That person is on vacation in Florida."

I said, "You need to call them, because I came here specifically for this reason."

The nurse called her, and she said, "I think he misunderstood me. The VA doesn't pay for partial medication. We either do it all or none of it."

I asked the lady that was there, "What do I need to do for you to do it all?"

She said, "Have you ever considered going to NIH?"

I said, "What is that?"

She said, "National Institute of Health in Maryland."

D. Frank said, "Yeah, I have heard of them."

She said, "Go over there, and see if you qualify."

Before we went to NIH, I was scheduled to be back in Charlotte at Carolina Medical Center to have a CAT scan of both my kidneys. The nurse told me to drink this liquid.

They said, "You are going to have to take a series of blood tests every thirty minutes."

They drew some blood, and then I had to drink this stuff—sixteen ounces—and go into another room and drink another thing of liquid, and then they ran dye through my kidneys to check them out.

They did all of that, and then when I was leaving, the lady who checked me out said, "You might have a little slight diarrhea from that chemical."

I couldn't even get out of Charlotte—it was pretty crazy.

I called her back and said, "I ought to strangle you all. You got me running back and forth to the bathroom. You didn't tell me that stuff would do that to me."

I went back to Washington, and my brother and I went to the NIH in Maryland. We told them we were both veterans, that we wanted to do a kidney transplant, and that I was a perfect match. They jumped right on it. The doctor said he needed to interview me.

I interviewed with the doctor. He asked me if I had ever had an MRI. I thought about it and I said, "I don't think so."

"If you had ever had one, you would always remember it," he said. "The first thing we are going to do is an MRI on your entire body."

He told me to be there at five o'clock in the morning for the MRI. I got there at about 4:30 a.m., and the ladies told me go up and eat a little breakfast because they weren't quite ready for me. What they didn't know was that I shouldn't have been eating breakfast. I ate breakfast and had a big cup of coffee.

One of the ladies came up a little later and said, "Okay, we are ready for you."

The technician had me in the MRI machine, and every time he told me to hold my breath and then breathe out, the coffee moved up, toward my throat.

The technician said "Just one more, just one more."

When he got done, the coffee was almost at my throat. I thought how embarrassing it would be if I threw up in the MRI machine and all over myself.

The doctors at NIH told me they were going to do the transplant in December.

We checked into the hospital, and my brother's white blood cell count was out of whack. He had gotten an infection from the dialysis using a rubber kidney because they were using the same artificial kidney on more than one person. They sent me home for the first time.

The second time I came to do the transplant, my brother was having trouble with his knee. He was putting a heating pad on the knee to bring the swelling down; his knee was killing him. He went to work preaching the night before we went into the hospital.

I said to him, "What are you doing? You are going for a transplant tomorrow. You don't need to be preaching tonight."

That night, he put his heating pad on. I told him that he should put a wet towel in the microwave and let it get warm, then put it on his leg, but someone had given him a heating pad. He thought he could put it on really tightly and make the whole problem go away by the next day, but all it actually did was blister it instead of making it better.

At the hospital, they said, "Your brother's white blood cell count is off again. We just can't understand it."

I said, "Well, have you looked at his knee?"

They checked his knee, came back in, cut my armband off, and told me to go home.

They told me to come back to NIH to have another test run on me. They did a colonoscopy.

The doctor said, "This is the deal: I am going to put your brother in the hospital, and I am going to get him healthy. Once I get him healthy, I am going to call you. I don't want to put your perfectly good kidney in him and have him kill it because he's not healthy."

I came back home, and people asked me, "What are you doing? Aren't you afraid something might happen?" In my line of work, there was always the chance of getting hurt.

I said, "No. I'm not doing anything to put myself at risk, where my life would be in jeopardy. Nothing I'm doing is going to hinder me from helping to save my brother."

THE PROPHECY
COMES TO PASS

A RIGHT TURN TO GOD

Prior to me going visiting the hospital for the second time, I met a Christian lady, Miss Ross, who worked at the telephone company. I was in paying a bill one day, and I told her what I was going to do, and she asked, "Is it okay that I put you on our prayer list? My sister lives in Charlotte, and I live here in Lancaster, and we want to pray for you and your brother."

While I knew the transplant would have to be done, my mother believed just the opposite. She said, "No, you don't need to worry about that, because God is going to heal his kidneys. You aren't going to have to have that transplant. God isn't going to put both of my sons on the operating table."

I told her, "God has a plan for doing this transplant. I can't explain it right now, but I know God has a plan."

She said, "I don't care what you think the plan is. I am telling you that God isn't going to put me through that."

I thought, *We have got to get Mom on our side.* Mom said I was just a baby Christian compared to her, that she had known the Lord a lot longer than I had, and she knew what God could do.

We still prepared for the transplant, and we still worked to get mom on our side.

The doctor said he would call me the week before the transplant, once my brother's health improved enough.

While I waited to receive the call from the doctor, my tour of duty as on-call investigator had come up. I was called out on a case in the middle of Wednesday night and into early Thursday morning. A couple was separated, and a friend of the wife had the husband's Lexus and a motorcycle at her house. He claimed he was over there as a friend, and he was waiting for his buddies to come and pick him up. While he was waiting for his buddies, an unknown person came over, poured fluid all over the Lexus and the motorcycle, and set them both on fire. The fire department was called to extinguish the fire.

Upon my arrival, the husband called and left a message on the answering machine that said, "What do you think about that pretty paint job?"

I figured right then that he was my suspect. I didn't really have to look any further. It was three o'clock in the morning, and decided I would just come back the next day and take pictures of the car.

I went home and then went back to work in the evening. The way our rotation schedule worked is that when I was on call, I worked from Friday evening to Friday morning of the following week.

Since I was going to be off the following Friday, I had my phone bill in the car to pay it. I was also going to take pictures of the burned vehicle from the night before. I got my camera and stuff together and put them in my car. I was driving a Ford Taurus at the time.

On my way from the sheriff's office, I was traveling west on Arch Street. I was planning to make a left, go down Market Street and then to Highway 200 toward where this incident took place.

When I got to the light at Arch and Market, I tried to make a left turn, but my car wouldn't go left. I tried everything. I tried with all my might to turn my car left, and the Spirit said, "Go by the phone company," which required that I make a right turn.

I said, "To the phone company?"

The Spirit said, "Yes."

When I agreed to go to the phone company, I could turn my steering wheel with one finger. The car started going right. I was driving down Market Street, and I said to the Spirit, "I am going to go through the drive-through."

He said, "No, you need to go inside."

I said, "I am going through the drive-through."

He said, "Why are you arguing with me?"

I said, "I will go inside."

I went inside and paid my phone bill. After paying the bill, I took a couple of steps from the counter, and I couldn't move. It was like I was frozen on the carpet. My feet acted as though I were glued to the carpet. I literally could not move.

I stood there with the receipt in my hand, and I said, "Lord, I have been obedient. I came in here and paid the phone bill. What do you want me to do?"

Then, Miss Ross walked out of her office about thirty feet away. She saw me, and in amazement, she made a gasp. It startled me when she did that.

She said, "Don't go anywhere; I need to speak to you."

I thought, *I can't go anywhere because I am planted on this carpet.*

She said, "I've got a customer." When she finished with her customer, she motioned for me to come to her desk. At that point, I was released from the carpet, so I went to her desk. I sat down, and she said, "Look, I got a message from God for you through my sister."

At that point, I was about to have a heart attack. I was wondering what she was about to tell me. She said it was so powerful that I had to write it down. My heart was beating fast. She opened her briefcase and took out a piece of paper. I watched her shaking, and my heart was really pounding.

She began to read, "God said, 'You are going to be pierced on your right side, and you will have an open wound for mankind, and you will live and not die.'" I just started boohooing.

She said, "Wait a minute. God also said that he could hardly bear it when they hung His Son on the cross, that his Son was pierced in His right side—that His Son has an open wound for mankind and will continue to live and not die."

We both started crying tears of joy.

I said, "Wait a minute, Miss Ross. How long have you known this?"

She said, "I couldn't tell you unless the Spirit brought you in here."

I said, "Wow, you wouldn't believe he nearly dragged me in here."

Leaving there, it felt like I was walking on a cloud. I had a surreal feeling of joy.

When I made it outside, I called my brother. I said, "D. Frank, you are not going to believe what happened."

I told him about the meeting and the message I just received from God. He said, "We have got to call mother."

My brother called her, and we had a three-way phone conversation with her. My mother started crying—all three of us were crying on the phone. My mother said, "That's the confirmation I have been waiting for. If God can handle His Son hanging on the cross, then I can handle two of my own sons being operated on at the same time."

I was getting prepared for the operation, and people were asking me, "Man, are you worried about what is going to happen?"

"No, God is in control of this whole situation. I just have to make sure I don't do anything to jeopardize my life, like getting shot or chasing someone and increasing my potential for getting hurt. I have got to stay healthy."

For a whole year, I had to stay healthy. I had to be prepared to leave at any moment to do the transplant.

Finally, the doctor called me and said, "I want you to be in Maryland on April second. Check in at the National Institute of Health in Bethesda on April third, and I want to do the transplant on April fourth."

I said, "Sounds great. Let's make this thing happen."

While I was up there, they made me drink this stuff called "golightly." Boy, believe me, it makes you go lightly. My family came to the hospital. My mother didn't like riding elevators, but our rooms were on the eleventh floor, so she asked God to give her the strength to ride the elevator, and He did.

When I got to the hospital on April third to check in, they said, "We got all your results back. You are 100 percent healthy and are good to go. Your brother is now healthy, and we are going to be able to do the transplant. All we need to do is take one more X-ray of your left kidney. You will sign for your left kidney, and on April fourth at four a.m., you are going to be sedated. Then, at 4:30 a.m., we are going to take out your eleventh rib and remove your left kidney."

I asked them if they were going to put my eleventh rib back, and they said, "No, you won't even miss it."

I said, "Yes, I will, because you told me you were going to take it."

As planned, at 4 a.m. on the fourth of April, they came into my room. They asked me how I had slept, and I responded, "Like a baby."

They wheeled me down to the operating room on the ninth floor. They strapped me down, and we were getting ready to do the operation when the doctor stood over me and said, "Mr. Waiters, we have a problem."

I said, "Goodness, you have got to be kidding me. You told me you were going to do this for my brother. You told me he was in good shape."

He said, "Whoa, it's not your brother."

I said, "Wait a minute. You have run every test known to man on me. CAT scans, upper GI, lower GI, MRI. You told me I was in perfect shape; that I was in good health."

He said, "Well, you know the left kidney you were going to give us? We don't want it."

I said, "What's wrong with it?"

The doctor said, "You have two ventricles."

I said, "What does that mean?"

He said, "You have *three* kidneys."

"*Three* kidneys?"

"Yes. We don't want your left kidney, we want your right one."

At that point, the nurse said, "He can't sign for the right kidney. He has been sedated."

The doctor asked, "Where is your wife?"

"I told her to stay in Washington."

"What about your mother?"

"I told her to do the same."

"Well, what's the phone number?" So I told him.

One of the doctors said, "Wow, he knew that number pretty well. He doesn't sound that sedated to me."

They stepped out of the room to have a little conference. When they came back in, the doctor said, "Can you sign for your right kidney?'

I said, "Sure."

They unstrapped my arm and held a clipboard up for me so I could sign for my right kidney. Once I signed, they put me under, and I was out.

About 4:30 that evening, the doctors woke me up and said, "Everything went great. Your brother is doing well. You came through it like a champ."

The day after the transplant, I was up and walking through the hall. At the same time, my doctor, who was an army doctor, was walking through the doors. I walked up to him, and he just stopped and shook his head. The closer I got to him, the more he shook his head.

I said to the doctor, "What's wrong?"

He said, "I don't believe you."

I said, "What don't you believe?"

He said, "You're up walking. No one is up walking the day after a transplant. Do you know how many of these things I have done? I have never seen anyone walking the next day."

I said, "I was told the faster I started moving, the faster I could get out of here."

He said, "You know, there are four significant things that happened to you. First of all, do you know what the odds are of a perfect match?"

I said, "No, sir."

He said, "Fourteen million to one. Do you know what the odds are of having three kidneys?"

I said, "No, sir."

He said, "We don't either. You are a pretty big man, but we only had to do a twelve-inch incision to remove your eleventh rib. It is awesome for you to be walking the next day. I know you are a big, bad Marine and a deputy sheriff, but I believe you are some kind of an angel. The Lord has really blessed you."

I said, "No, I'm just trying to get well so I can get out of the hospital."

I went back to my room, and it hit me—*You are going to be pierced on the right side.*

That's when I realized I had been pierced on my right side, and that God had already made the plan for all of this to happen.

I didn't know it at the time, but when you have a major operation, they put your intestines to sleep so they aren't moving around while you are being operated on. Well, your intestines have to wake up, too.

A lot of times, walking around will wake them up. My intestines had not awakened, and the first thing they did after surgery was pull the catheter out.

The nurse said, "I need to get a urine specimen from you."

I couldn't make urine for anything. She came back in and said, "I want to give you an incentive to make urine," and placed the catheter on the tray next to my bed.

I was doing everything I could think of to make urine. I put my hand under running water and just let the water run. I would have done anything to make sure they didn't have to put that catheter back in. Finally, I was able to make enough urine for them to run a test.

My intestines didn't wake up until after the second day.

The anesthetist came in while the nurse was in. He said, "I can wake up your intestines."

I looked at him and said, "How are you going to do it?"

He handed me a little bottle and said, "I am going to give you a shot, and it is going to wake them up. Whenever they do operations on people who can't get up and walk around, we give them this shot, and it wakes up their intestines."

He gave me this shot, and about an hour later, it sounded like dinosaurs were waking up. I was making crazy noises. Sure enough, my intestines woke up, and off to the bathroom I went. I have never experienced anything like that. Three days later, I went home.

My brother wanted to go home, but they told him he had to stay a little longer. I went to my brother's house in Washington,

DC to recover, because the doctor told me it would be a while before I could travel. In the meantime, my family had gone back to South Carolina. After a day at my brother's house, my mother called me crying.

She said, "A mortgage company is going to take my sister's house."

My mother's sister was eighty-four years old, and my mother told me a mortgage company was going to take her house. I told her it had to be a mistake; that her house had been paid in full for years. I told her to let me call the tax office and talk to the clerk to see what was going on. I told her that I would take care of it, which made her feel a whole lot better.

During this same time, my cousin Sadie, who was one of my mother's best friends, had passed away, and they were making preparations for the funeral. I was going to try and come home for her funeral, even though I still wasn't in any shape to travel.

My brothers and sisters had a plan. They were going to strap me in the van and put a bunch of pillows around me to let me travel. They tried to lay me in the backseat, but it was pretty difficult. The spot where my rib had been removed was still very sore, and every bump the van hit, I felt it, and it hurt.

They put me in the passenger's seat, and they put pillows around me and strapped me in. I was able to ride home and make it to the funeral.

A week or so after that, my brother came home.

THE WITNESS

THE AFTERMATH

A year after later, I went back to Washington and did blood work. I thought the nurses were going to just draw some blood, but one nurse asked me, "What movie do you want to see?"

I said, "What do you mean what movie do I want to see?"

The nurse said, "You can pick a movie, because it is going to be about three hours or so."

It was kind of like being on dialysis. They removed my platelets, took my blood, and analyzed my plasma, then put my blood back. My brother had the same test done, and our vitals were 0.1 percent from being identical. My brother was doing great. I was doing great.

It was kind of funny that I was pierced on the right side, because that is the same side where I wear my gun. When I went back to work about six weeks after the operation, my right side was really sore. It took a while to heal.

I was concerned about still being sore after six weeks and how long would it take to heal, so I called the hospital and asked the doctors. They said I would be completely healed in six months. I was still a little sore after six months, so they said it would probably take a year for me to totally heal. In a year, I was pretty much healed.

Right before we went in for the operation, I remember someone said to me, "You are about to do a transplant. How do you feel?"

I said, "Well, I feel good."

"Are you afraid?"

I thought about it. I was not afraid. God had removed any kind of fear from me. It was like it was His plan, and then I had confirmation from God that I would be pierced on the right side and live. That even gave my mom satisfaction in the knowledge that God wanted us to do this.

Then, God said this to me: *I want you to let the world know that even in 2006, I am still performing miracles."*

I thought, *Yeah, we have to do this.*

We did interviews about the transplant—about the fact that I had three kidneys and that I was a perfect match—in several newspapers. The *County Line,* a local quarterly magazine, ran the story on the front page. That story was up for the article of the year. The Lancaster newspaper did an article and another paper did an article on it. Several people called and wanted to talk to me. I met a lot of different people, and every time I talked to someone new, I had to talk about the transplant.

A Piercing Feeling

When Mel Gibson released *The Passion of the Christ,* I was awe-struck. When I went to see the movie, I could hardly wait to get to the scene where Jesus was pierced in His right side. In the movie, Jesus is in the square, and the crowd is beating Him. The whip they used to beat Him had a claw on the end of it, and when that claw hit His side, Jesus said, "Ah!" That was the first time He made any sound from the pain.

As the movie progressed, one scene showed Jesus hanging on the cross. One of the men involved in the crucifixion rode by on a donkey. He said something along the lines of, "Let me see you get off the cross since you are so bad," to Jesus.

Right after that, Jesus passed away.

When Jesus died, they said God shed a tear. A single teardrop fell, but it was like an earthquake.

One of the men said, "Hit them in the knees and make sure they are dead. So they will bleed out." He ran up to one of the guys and hit him in the knees, and then he looked at Jesus and said, "He's already dead."

They said, "Make sure. Pierce him in his side."

When the guard struck Jesus in the side, blood splattered over him. Realizing what he had done, he fell to his knees and asked God to forgive him.

During this scene, something happened to me. When the guard stabbed Him in the side, it felt like someone stabbed me in my side. I exclaimed, "Ah!" I couldn't say anything. Walking out of the movie theater, everybody was just talking about the movie, but I was in awe. I didn't know what to do. What I had just experienced was unbelievable.

A short time later, I took my mother to the movie, and even though I knew that scene was coming, I still felt the same—that I had been pierced in my side.

Then, Jesus came to me and said, *I am telling you that I need you to let the world know that I am still performing miracles, even today. You have to let the world know. You have to be the witness.*

LISTEN WITH YOUR HEART

January 1, 2001, I went back on patrol as a sergeant. I started to get back to a regular routine. My brother and I had come through the surgery in April of the year before, and things were finally getting back to normal. I worked with a young man, the lieutenant on my shift, Roy Hardin.

Roy was a hardworking guy, but he was overweight and smoked a lot. He'd had heart problems, and he had a heart attack at one point. His doctor told him he needed a pacemaker, but he didn't want to take the time off to get the pacemaker.

I told him it would be better to get the pacemaker installed and live longer than to not get it and die sooner.

The way our shifts worked, we each worked four twelve-hour days then were off for seven days. Then, we'd come back and work four nights and be off three days. After that, we would work three days and be off one day, then work three nights and be off three days.

The four early days were pretty rough. I had to get up at four in the morning, do roll call at 5:15, and start taking calls at 5:30. I would work all the way up until six o'clock or 6:30, depending on how much paperwork I had to do or how many calls I had taken that day.

Roy and I had worked the weekend for some other guys, then we had to work our four early days. That meant we would each work six straight twelve-hour days.

On top of that, Roy was working six hours over the end of his shift for another officer, and I was covering for him in the mornings so he wouldn't have to get up at 4:00 a.m. Instead, he'd come in around six.

On a Wednesday night, the Spirit came to me and told me to tell Roy that if he continued working like this, he was going to have a heart attack and die.

The Lord was adamant about me expressing this to Roy. The following Thursday, was going to be our last day. We had roll call. Roy had worked the previous night until midnight. Then, he came in early—he was a workaholic.

I said, "Roy, what are you doing?"

He said, "I'm trying to pay my hospital bill."

"Man, that hospital bill will be there when you're dead and gone. You're going to work yourself to death. You can't keep working these crazy hours. You've worked six straight days in a row, plus you worked six hours over on three of the six days. You can't keep doing this. You're going to burn yourself out."

I told him I had something to tell him that the Lord had told me to reveal to him.

He gave me a look that said, *Oh my God! What is it?* Then, he said, "Let's get everybody out onto the street, and then you and I will sit down and talk." We got everybody out and went into the library.

We sat down, and I said, "The Lord told me to tell you that if you keep working like you're working, you're going to have a heart attack and die. I want you to promise me you're not going to work over tonight. You're going to go home to get some rest. You're working too much."

He said, "Okay, I'm not going to work over today. When we get off today, I'm all done."

"You promise me that."

"Yeah."

I had ordered a television from Sears, and it had come in that day. They told me I could pick it up at four o'clock.

I called Roy and said, "Man, I got a television that came in, and I can pick it up at four. I'm going to take off a couple of hours early and bail out of here."

I forgot to emphasize to him not to work anymore.

I picked up the TV, went home, and installed everything. I went to sleep about nine o'clock, and the phone rang at about 10:30. It was the dispatcher, and she was crying.

I said, "What's wrong?"

She said, "Roy's dead."

I said, "Roy's dead? Roy's not working!"

She said, "Yeah, he worked over."

"I told Roy not to work over!"

"He was on a call, and he had a heart attack walking up the driveway."

"Lord, have mercy."

I don't know how much plainer the Lord could have made it. I told Roy what the Lord told me, but he didn't listen, and he died.

We had Roy's funeral, and it was pretty tough to deal with, especially since I had just talked to him about his work. He died doing what he loved to do, but he basically killed himself because he wasn't taking care of himself.

I found out later he had run out of his heart medication, but he had been working so much that he hadn't taken the time to get his medicine refilled.

Throughout the next five years, I worked with a couple of other lieutenants, and I worked every shift we had. Each and every one of those lieutenants had their quirks, but when you've got God in your life, it doesn't matter who you work with or what you deal with.

The Bible reminds me that whatever state I'm in, I can be content. I am able to handle whatever situation is handed to me.

THE REASON WHY

I wrote this book to let the world know that God is still a miracle worker. I am a living witness, and God has commissioned me to let the world know. He provided miracles for my brother—a transplant and a healthy life. Six years later, my brother is still doing well.

The Lord chose me as a vehicle to re-establish that He can and will perform a miracle for you. I want everyone to know that God is very good. He will answer any prayer you have. At all times, if you put Him first in your life, there is nothing in this world you can't accomplish.

Jesus told us, *I will not leave you comfortless. Just call on Him.* [John 14:18]

I wrote a poem thirty years ago, when I was nineteen years old. I was sitting on a mountain in California, and the Lord brought this poem to me:

● ●

We are what we are, and we can be whatever we want to be.
For I am not you; and you are not me.
Don't judge me for what I used to be
For I may change, for nothing stays the same.
The rain comes from the clouds,
And the sun, lights up the sky,
And for everything there is a reason,
And there's a reason for everything.

● ●

I live my life under those premises. We do change as we get older. We get wiser. We have a tendency to change for the better. We all must have a little rain in our lives, but we also have the sunshine. The flowers and trees need both elements to survive. There's a reason for everything—that is the truth about life, and the truth will never change. It doesn't matter how many sides there are to a story—your side, his side, or her side—because there is always the truth, and that is the side that will always stand.

Sometimes we question things. We ask, "Why did this happen to me? Why was I chosen to do this? Why did this happen in my family?"

There are reasons behind these things, and sometimes it is not for us to analyze them but just go with it.

When I think back, I can count five people I was really close to who passed away.

The first person who passed away was my uncle when I went to Parris Island in 1976, followed by my grandmother on my mother's side in 1978. My Uncle Ray died in 1981; then it was my father in 1983. My younger brother, Harry, died in 1995.

When Harry died, I was so angry, just as I was angry with God when my father passed away. I couldn't understand. My father was a Christian and had done a lot of good things. He was a true father and a true Christian. He was in the church. I didn't understand how could God just take him away like that.

My father always told me that he didn't want to suffer, and he didn't. He was in the hospital, and he came home for about a week. When they rushed him back to the hospital, he died. He said he didn't want to be a burden on anyone.

Twelve years later, when my baby brother passed away, I said, "God what are you doing to me?" When my father passed away, God told me to read the book of Job, so I read the book of Job, but I didn't understand what He wanted me to do.

When my baby brother died, I was crying and upset, and I thought, *What is going on here? God, what are you doing?*

God said, "Go to the book of Job."

I said, "I have already read the book of Job. What do you want me to understand about the book of Job?"

I went back to the book of Job, and I read it again and again, and then it came to me what God wanted me to see. In the book of Job, Job's children were all killed, and one servant came back to tell him. All his sheep were consumed by fire, and all his camels were stolen. This all happened in one day.

First, my father died, and then twelve years later, my brother. These things happened over a period of time, and they were tragic, but they hadn't happened at the same time. God hadn't put them both on our hearts at one time. I don't know anyone personally that could handle Job's kind of tragedy all at one time.

REMEMBERING HARRY

Now, I remember Harry as he should be remembered—as we knew him, not in sadness.

Harry was a quirky little guy we all knew and loved. Harry was funny. He had the innate ability to turn negative situations into positive. This little guy could talk his way out of anything, and if there was humor in a situation, he could find it.

I remember when the Marine Corps gave me orders that I had been stationed in California, Harry said, "I bet you are going to be peeling potatoes." He saw in the movies where soldiers on mess duty had to peel potatoes. I didn't say anything. I just let the remark fly.

When I got to California, there was a delay in getting the school started, so the CO said, "What we are going to do is put some on mess duty. He'll work in the cafeteria, and some of you will be on guard duty, and you can rotate. You can do this until school starts."

They started me out on mess duty. They asked if I wanted day or night mess. I took night mess. The first thing they asked the group on night mess was, "Who wants to peel potatoes?"

I thought about what Harry said, and I told them, "I am not peeling potatoes. I will do anything else, but I am not peeling potatoes. Let me crack eggs."

I cracked so many eggs, it took a long time before I ate another egg, but I thought of Harry cracking on me about peeling potatoes and I kept cracking eggs.

He was one of those characters everybody loved. Harry made an impact on everyone he met. When his son was in the hospital in Charleston, Harry made such an impact on the staff. He stayed the entire time his son was hospitalized, encouraging everyone else. He was just being his jovial self. A day or two before his son was scheduled to come home, Harry died in that hospital—not as a patient, but as a friend.

There are a lot of people today who lose money on the stock market, and they kill themselves and others along the way. I have learned to be a more patient person; a more understanding father, uncle, and individual; a friend; and a police officer. I guess I try to carry myself in a way that guarantees I will see my father, brother, grandmother and uncle again.

THE CONCLUSION

As I have traveled through life, I have learned to be more in tune with God. I understand that we all have a guardian angel. It is up to us to accept the things that God tells us and realize He knows what is best for us. We need to trust God and try to keep a positive attitude.

When I got married, we had a singlewide mobile home. As time went by, we decided to get a bigger home. I had already purchased a pretty nice home in Florida while I was stationed there. The mobile home that we were living in at the time was one that I bought while in the Marines, and the Marine Corps had moved and set it up for us. I let my brothers live in it, then rented it out until I returned to live in it myself. We stayed in it for a while, then decided to purchase a bigger home.

Shortly after the transplant in 2000, God blessed my wife and me when we were able to close the deal on a new home. Within six months, we were in the home—a beautiful, three-bedroom home with three baths, and a two-car garage. It is a dream come true, sitting on a beautiful piece of property with a big yard and front and back porches. We only had to bring $75.00 to the closing. I know God is good. There is no way man would create that kind of opportunity for me.

I realize those are just material things, but God did something else for me for which I am truly grateful. I mentioned this briefly earlier, but I want to say it again. God brought my son back from Baghdad when many did not get to come home again. It is amazing to think about all the things God has done for me.

In the quiet times of my day, usually when I am on my way to work at five a.m., or on my way home from work, I talk with the Lord. I often relive some of the moments and things my father shared with me.

He taught me a couple of things about family. One day, my father took me for a walk in the woods. He picked up a handful of dirt and said, "Don't let this steal your soul." I gathered from this that he was telling me to remember what's important.

My great-grandfather purchased that land, and my dad told me, "Don't let this land, my brothers, or your family cause you to lose sight of what's important."

My great-grandfather had to make some decisions regarding the land when he became ill. Since then, there has been a little rift between the heirs of Can Waiters because of his choices. I would love to have met my great-grandfather. He was one of fourteen brothers and seven sisters. A prominent figure in the community at the signing of the Emancipation Proclamation, it was his will that as long as a Waiters was living, he or she would always have a place to live.

Today, I am still trying to carry out his wishes by preserving the land and taking care of the family.

Some nonbelievers may read this book and question its authenticity, question whether the miracles in this book really happened. Yes, they did. Each and every one of the miracles happened. I stand on the side of truth. It has been an awesome opportunity, bringing this to you. Of the billions of people in this world, God chose me to be a messenger for Him. I am grateful.

As I See It

Rev. D. Frank Waiters

I often wondered why me, why I was the one afflicted. The answer came back, "Why not you?"

The Bible states that God would not allow us to be tempted above that we are able to bear. Otherwise, He would with the temptation make a way for our escape from the temptation.

Throughout this whole ordeal, my mother, brothers, sisters, wife, and family members went through a great deal of preparation, but none more than my donor, my brother Kevan, who had to make such an important decision. I am so thankful he made the decision and happy about how our lives have turned out.

He was the brother the doctors said might not make it. Of the eleven brothers and sisters in my family, he was the most difficult pregnancy our mother experienced, but the Lord had other plans for him. He operates on a different level than the rest of us.

He has a drive that I have not seen in any of my other brothers and sisters.

Kevan is like our dad when he needs to be and like our mom when he needs to be. My dad was a realist and my mom an optimist, and I find my brother exhibits both those characteristics. However grateful I am for the way things have turned out, I often think about that dreaded *What if?*

Because I have a transplanted kidney, my doctors have told me I have to do certain things and that if I don't, things won't be favorable for me. I am healthy today, and I am feeling great, but I will admit that sometimes it has been a struggle. I'm not that different from most people; we don't always do the things we are supposed to do, but I have learned that just because you *can* doesn't mean you *should*, and vice versa.

One thing is for sure, though. I will not have put my family through such an ordeal and then not take care of my health.

Whether I could have changed anything in my past to prevent kidney failure, I really don't know, but I will change my habits to prevent any more destruction. I take God at His word—healing belongs to me. His word is not for me alone, but for everyone. I have learned to live the way God instructs me to live, to have the life He has given me. God allowed me to make it through this, so I will be a spokesperson for Him.

Someone may need to hear this story so they can relate to it. In fact, God gave us His living word, the Bible, so that we can relate to it. Once you realize there is purpose attached to your being, you will view life more objectively, do things more freely, and give it your all. Somebody needs your experiences. Your life is an assignment.

I see the struggles my wife and I have come through as learning vehicles. As a person not used to having others help me, I have learned how to receive from my family. They have been a great support system for me then and now. No man is an island, and no man stands alone—this is a truth I really had to embrace. The kidney disease is the condition I could see, but there were so many other healings that took place that weren't visible to the eye.

I am grateful today that the Lord called me, protected me, and kept me while I was going through those down periods. We have all seen and witnessed Him working on our behalf. I thank Him for everything. The Bible says the eyes of the Lord go throughout all the earth, seeking someone to show himself strong on behalf of His people.

He has allowed us to come this far. I won't turn around.

My assignment now is to tell people about the goodness of God and what He has done for my family, and not just my family, but all the families of the world.

In addition to that, my cry now is, "Lord, what else do you want me to do? Use me, Lord. Here I am. I want you to use me."

I know for sure that there is a definite purpose for my existence, and that is, among other things, to bring glory to God. I try to express it in my songwriting, and even just as I meet people. God has fixed it so that I have acquaintances all over the world. I am glad I can tell the world, "A charge to keep I have—and a God to glorify."

I am no longer focusing on the negative things that have occurred throughout my past. The enemy tried to destroy me through failed marriages, sickness, disgruntled parishioners, the loss of my dad and my baby brother, and my wife Nita having brain surgery. Look at us now—my wife is healed, I have a brand new kidney, and I am able to travel the world and just talk about Jesus. My mother is still with us; she is clothed in her right mind; my brother Kevan, who donated the kidney, is doing well; my family is blessed; and our children are blessed. We went through the storm and the rain, but we made it. Thanks be to God, who gives us the victory!

Appendix

Waiters Family and the Number Three

My oldest brother is Ernest, born June 7, 1942; my second sister is Irene James Carr, born November 24, 1943. My third sister is Janice Dixon, and Janice was born November 19, 1945. My next sibling is Donald Frank Waiters, born December 30, 1947. The next is Rayford Joe Waiters—they call him Joe Ray. He was born December 16, 1949, which happens to be my father's birthday also, December 16, 1921. My next sister is Carolyn McKinney, and Carolyn was born February 9, 1952. Next is Larry Darnell Waiters, and Larry was born December 13, 1954. Next is my sister Denise Allen. Denise was born April 7, 1956. Then comes me, Kevan. I was born July 25, 1957. I was the baby for about five-and-a-half years, and along came Ginger Ann Waiters. Ginger was born January 30, 1963. The baby boy, Harry Evangelist Waiters, who is now deceased, was born April 28, 1964. Harry passed away March 30, 1995.

My mother had children in groups of three. The first group of three was one boy and two girls, the second was two boys and one girl, and the third was one boy, one girl, and another boy. Then, she had a girl and a boy.

My father had three fingers cut off in an accident on his job, and I just happened to be three years old when that happened.

When we were milking the cows before we went to school in the mornings, three tits were used for milking, and the other was left to her calf.

My mother told me that she and three of her seven sisters were pregnant and had miscarriages when my grandfather passed away.

Three drivers quit my first bus driver's route before I got it.

The three things I wanted to accomplish in life: travel and see the world, continue my education, and get paid while doing it.

When I went into the military, we had three phases of training.

In an Initial Strength Test, where we had to do a minimum of three pull-ups.

I had three days of light duty from a stress fracture while stationed at Parris Island.

I asked God to let it rain so I could attend rifle qualification with my unit. It rained three days.

I was able to get out of the last three days of physical training before graduation due to a nerve injury that caused my leg to go haywire.

When I was first stationed in Charleston, they had a three percent reenlistment rate.

I was an E-3 during my weaponry training. Three of us were lying in the prone position for this training.

During Hurricane David's reign of destruction, we stayed in our barracks three days, eating our sea rations.

I have three children: Marie, Brandon, and Keri.

D. Frank had three wives.

I held a supervisory position for three years in Jackson-ville, Florida.

When looking for a potential donor for my brother's kidney transplant, the three of us lived in South Carolina.

My son joined the Marine Corps in 2003 and has spent six years in the Marines, three of which were served in Iraq.

That's just to mention a few. The second greatest miracle of my life makes the number three very significant.